William George Ward

The authority of doctrinal decisions

William George Ward

The authority of doctrinal decisions

ISBN/EAN: 9783741176081

Manufactured in Europe, USA, Canada, Australia, Japa

Cover: Foto ©Andreas Hilbeck / pixelio.de

Manufactured and distributed by brebook publishing software
(www.brebook.com)

William George Ward

The authority of doctrinal decisions

THE AUTHORITY

OF

DOCTRINAL DECISIONS.

THE AUTHORITY

OF

DOCTRINAL DECISIONS

WHICH ARE NOT DEFINITIONS OF FAITH,

CONSIDERED IN A SHORT SERIES OF ESSAYS REPRINTED FROM

"THE DUBLIN REVIEW."

BY

WILLIAM GEORGE WARD, D.Ph.

LONDON:

BURNS, LAMBERT, AND OATES,

17 PORTMAN STREET, PORTMAN SQUARE.

1866.

COX AND WYMAN,

ORIENTAL, CLASSICAL, AND GENERAL PRINTERS

GREAT QUEEN STREET, LONDON, W.C.

DEDICATION.

TO THE MOST REVEREND HENRY EDWARD,
LORD ARCHBISHOP OF WESTMINSTER.

My dear Lord Archbishop,

THERE is nothing which you have more earnestly taught us, than that the interests of "truth" come before those of "peace"; or rather, that all Christian peace, really such, is based on Christian truth. Nor have you been less emphatic in inculcating, that there is no security for religious truth, except in the most humble and unreserved submission to the Church, on all matters which are related ever so remotely to faith and morals. Since, therefore, in the following pages, I have treated a small portion of this large subject, it is not unnatural that I should have solicited you to accept its dedication. I esteem your compliance with that request as one of those kindnesses, which during late years you have shown me in such abundance, and for which I shall ever be most grateful.

I trust I may consider that, in according this permission, you have given your blessing both to me and to my little work; and I sincerely hope that you will approve its contents.

That you may be long spared us to exhibit and teach that devoted loyalty to the Holy See, which is our one protection against the misbelief and unbelief of our unhappy age, is the constant prayer,

My dear Lord Archbishop,

Of your Grace's dutiful and affectionate Servant,

WILLIAM GEORGE WARD.

PREFACE.

THOSE who differ most strongly from the views maintained in this volume, will be forward in admitting the extreme and inappreciable importance of the question at issue. They will be glad, therefore, to see collected in one, the arguments which I have been putting forward on it from time to time in the *Dublin Review*, for the last year and a half. In order that I may more facilitate reference to those arguments, I will here say a few words on the precise doctrine for which I have been contending; and also on the place held in my general reasoning by those respective Essays, which are here again presented to the public.

"There are two questions, totally distinct from each other, and requiring an examination altogether distinct:—the 'subject' and the 'object' of infallibility. When I am considering the former, I am considering who *possesses* infallibility; whether *e. g.* the Pope alone, or not without episcopal concurrence:

but when I am considering the latter, I am considering *over what objects* infallibility extends; whether *e. g.* it is confined to definitions of faith, or extends much further" (p. 192).

Now, with the former of these questions the present volume is not at all concerned. For myself, undoubtedly, I am of the Ultramontane school; and hold most confidently, that the Pope's declaration ex cathedrâ is at once and ipso facto the Church's infallible teaching. But hardly any part of these Essays is intended as an argument for Ultramontanism. On the contrary, I consider that all my reasoning, or very nearly all, possesses the same force for Gallicans as for Ultramontanes, if, wherever I speak of a Papal declaration, they will but add their characteristic qualification; if they will consider me to speak only of such a Papal declaration, as has been accepted expressly or tacitly by the Catholic Episcopate. I have expressed this, indeed, repeatedly throughout.

I am here, then, exclusively treating the "object" of infallibility. And on this I make three preliminary remarks. (1.) When it is said that the Pope issues some instruction ex cathedrâ, neither more nor less is meant than that he issues it *in his capacity of Universal Teacher.* (2.) It is admitted by all Catholics, that every instruction put forth by him ex cathedrâ, and accepted expressly or tacitly by the Episcopate, is infallibly true. (3.) It is also admitted by all Catholics without exception, that no instruction put forth by the Pope in any other capacity than that of Universal Teacher, possesses this divine promise of infallibility. It is plain, therefore, that to discuss the "object" of infallibility, is precisely to examine the question, in what cases the Pope speaks ex cathedrâ. On this question, three different opinions may be held by a Catholic, without the actual abandonment of his Catholic profession.

(1.) "The Pope speaks ex cathedrâ, only in his actual definitions of faith; in cases, that is, where he so teaches a doctrine, as to pronounce its contradictory *heretical*. Under such circumstances, he expressly or virtually *anathematises* the wilful upholders of that contradictory tenet."

(2.) "He speaks ex cathedrâ, whenever he formally and precisely instructs the flock to beware of certain tenets, as *theologically unsound;* even though he does not condemn them as actually *heretical*. But his Allocutions, Encyclicals, &c. &c. never contain any such formal and precise instruction: much less does any letter, formally addressed by him to an individual bishop. He never, therefore, speaks ex cathedrâ in Allocutions, Encyclicals, and the like; still less in any letter formally addressed to an individual bishop." This opinion will be found drawn out at greater length in pp. 40 and 44.

(3.) "Various official addresses of the Pope—such as Allocutions, Encyclicals, and the like—are not, even in form, addressed to one individual or one nation in the Church, rather than to another. All the doctrinal instructions contained in these addresses are ex cathedrâ. All the doctrinal *instructions*: not all the doctrinal *dicta;* because these latter may often be *obiter* dicta. Further, in many of the Pope's official letters, addressed formally to individual bishops, he also speaks ex cathedrâ."

This is the thesis which I accept myself. I will at once refer to pp. 42, 50, 51, 121-8, 130; but the one object of my volume is to illustrate and defend it.

Two lines of objection to this thesis are imaginable in the mouth of a Catholic, essentially different from each other.

It may imaginably be maintained, that the Pope and Ecclesia Docens *claim,* indeed, such infallibility, but that the claim is unfounded. In reply, however, to so extreme a suggestion, let the following consideration be duly weighed.

A Catholic, simply as such, holds the Church to be his one divinely appointed guide, on matters of faith and morals. But what question more undeniably appertains to faith, than the extent of infallibility? or what question more undeniably appertains to morals, than the inquiry whether to certain pronouncements that unreserved assent be due, which is legitimately claimed by an infallible instruction? To say, therefore, that she can teach wrongly on the issue discussed in this volume, is simply to say that she is *not* infallible within the sphere of faith and morals.

I have expressed, in p. 43, an argument substantially the same. "He who accepts Catholicism, by that very fact accepts the Ecclesia Docens as his guide to Heaven. Now, the Ecclesia Docens"—so much is admitted by the objector—"teaches that certain doctrines are infallibly true, as being integral parts of the Catholic Faith; and that certain others are infallibly true, as being indissolubly bound up with the former. On what imaginable ground can any one accept her testimony to the former class, while he rejects her testimony to the latter? If she is mistaken in considering herself infallible on one class of questions, how can he take her word for her infallibility on another?"

There are several Catholics perhaps who are, more or less unconsciously, imbued with such a notion as this; but I doubt if there is one, who will explicitly contemplate, and then deliberately embrace it. If there is such an one, he is altogether beyond the reach of any argument which I can adduce.

If any proposition in the world, then, is indubitable on Catholic principles, it is that the Church *possesses* whatever infallibility she *claims*. If the Pope claims a certain infallibility, every Ultramontane is bound in consistency to take his word for it; and if the Episcopate accepts that claim, not Ultramontanes only, but all Catholics, are likewise under the obligation of admitting it.

The issue, therefore, before us resolves itself into

one of fact. *Does* the Pope claim to teach doctrine ex cathedrâ in Allocutions, Encyclicals, and the like? and, surely, the most uncandid of men must perforce admit that he does, if he will but read with any attention the history of the "Mirari vos" (see pp. 54—63). And this of course is only one instance out of very many.

The articles, which I have written on this general question, are in almost every case occupied with other topics also; but I have retained those portions only, which bear on the present argument. And I will here briefly explain the ground, which they are respectively intended to cover.

In the first Essay I draw out what appears to me the "rationale" of those theological censures, which are less grave than that of heresy. I also call attention to the extremely large body of truths, which in one sense appertain to secular science; but which, as bearing indirectly on the Church's dogma, fall absolutely under the Church's infallible determination. The same Essay contains various other considerations, which will, I hope, be found useful preliminaries, to an apprehension of my general reasoning.

In the second Essay I have availed myself of F. Steccanella's guidance, for the purpose of pointing out the weight attached by the whole Catholic Episcopate to the Pope's solemn pronouncement on his civil princedom. They proclaim that, in consequence of that pronouncement, they are bound to accept, *as certain*, the whole doctrine therein contained. No fair person, I think, will doubt that they mean to express its "infallibility"; but I admit that neither that word, nor any precise equivalent, is found in their address.

In the third Essay, however, this omission is superabundantly supplied. That the doctrinal instructions of the "Mirari vos" are the infallible utterances of S. Peter's successor, is asserted again and again, in every variety of shape, whether by Gregory XVI. himself, or by Cardinal Pacca in his name. The Encyclical was solicited, both by Lamennais and by the French bishops, and also accepted by the latter, as an *infallible* decision of the controversies at issue (pp. 56, 61). Moreover, Lamennais himself recounts (p. 57) what murmurs rose against him among the body of French Catholics, when they began to suspect that he did not submit to it as infallibly true. I have further argued (p. 45), that all objections urged against the doctrinal infallibility of Encyclicals in general, apply with far greater force to this, than to any other which can be named.

In the same Essay I have also explained, to the best of my power, how far this doctrine of infallibility may legitimately be carried (pp. 50, 51); since undoubtedly no declarations possess this attribute, except those intended to teach the whole Church some doctrine. There is one relevant question, however, which I purposely reserved to a later period (see pp. 121-8); viz., what tests are available, to know whether some given letter, addressed formally to an individual bishop, is really a doctrinal instruction ex cathedrâ.

In the same Essay (which, indeed, I consider as containing the kernel of my reasoning more than all the rest put together) I have adduced various other arguments and testimonies, in behalf of my conclusion. Particularly I would draw attention to what I have urged (pp. 48, 49) on the intolerable intellectual tyranny which my opponents ascribe to the Church.

In the fourth Essay I have indicated briefly the vast amount of evidence, which establishes that the recent Encyclical and Syllabus were issued ex cathedrâ. It seems to me, indeed, that the whole subject has been invested with quite a new light, since their publication; and that that publication will hereafter rank as one of the most momentous epochs in the Church's whole annals. I am quite at a loss to imagine, since the history of their publication and reception has been known, how any Catholic can doubt, either that the Pope claimed infallibility for them, or that the Episcopate accepted that claim.

In the fifth Essay, I have recounted at much greater length the testimony of the French bishops to this infallibility (pp. 85-91). It is most observable, as I there point out, that they speak of this infallibility, not as of a doubtful or controvertible matter, but as of a doctrine quite rudimental—familiar to all Catholics—contained in the very Catechism. No bishop, it should be added, from one end of the Church to the other, has so much as publicly hinted a *doubt* of this infallibility. Among ourselves, both the Archbishop and the Bishop of Shrewsbury have expressly taught it as quite undeniable.

But the chief object of my fifth Essay has been the Church's infallibility in her magisterium. This is an extremely large question, and peculiarly important at this time; insomuch that to treat it at all satisfactorily would require a volume. Yet it seemed better not to omit the few remarks I had made on it; and the rather, because it is so very closely connected with my general theme. If the Church is infallible in her whole magisterium, she is infallible inclusively in that large body of explicit instruction, which she issues for the guidance of her children.

The sixth Essay gives an analysis of Dr. Murray's view on the same general theme as mine. His testimony on the agreement of theologians is especially important, as coming from one so intimately familiar with their works. It shows the very great importance which the question is now assuming, that he considers it so carefully and in so much detail. I cannot find any such treatment of it, in any earlier work on the Church with which I happen to be acquainted.

I was led to write the seventh and eighth Essays, by one plausible objection, which has been most prominently and repeatedly urged. "The Church cannot consider such decrees infallible; for Galileo's condemnation was one of them, and this she has tacitly revoked." I make with great ease the very obvious reply, that Galileo's condemnation was most certainly *not* one of these decrees; that there is not the most superficial pretence for saying that it was issued ex cathedrâ; and that many eminent contemporary Catholics, who most earnestly advocated its truth, yet expressly admitted its fallibility (pp. 131, 2; 159-162).

But it seemed far more satisfactory not to leave the matter there. The general question of doctrinal decrees, put forth by a Pontifical Congregation, is of great moment, and is closely connected with my main theme; and I thought it, therefore, far more satisfactory, to discuss it as well as I could. The conclusions which I advocate are these:—(1.) Such decrees, if promulgated by the Pope's express command, are probably ex cathedrâ. (2.) If they are not so promulgated, they are most certainly not sanctioned by him in his capacity of Universal Teacher; and if sanctioned by him at all, are so in his capacity of the Church's Ruler. (3.) Even in this case, however, we owe them interior assent; such as that with which a docile son accepts the paternal instructions: the same in kind, but far firmer in degree. (4.) Although it is most certain that these decrees have no promise of inerrancy, yet we may humbly hope that in fact God's Providence will always preserve them from error. This last opinion, however, I hold, of course, only as one piously probable; "and whenever a clear case of mistake is conclusively established, I shall of course change my mind." (5.) I am very confident, at all events, that Galileo's condemnation was no such case; but, on the contrary, that it afforded true doctrinal guidance to contemporary Catholics. In my last Essay (p. 196) I have explained the meaning of this statement, more clearly than I had done before.

I have thus been led to sum up briefly the general conclusions which I humbly advocate, on those various doctrinal dicta, which Popes may officially put forth (pp. 183-9).

As to the particular case of Galileo, my friend, F. Roberts, has advertised a criticism on my article, which may probably be appearing about the same time with this volume. His criticism will quite certainly contain many acute remarks, most clearly and candidly expressed. I confess I shall be surprised if he induces me to change my mind; but I will give his argument the most careful attention. That Galileo's condemnation was no pronouncement ex cathedrâ, is most absolutely certain. If, therefore, it were shown to have been (in any proper sense of the word) mistaken (see p. 199), the only result would be, that Catholics could not entertain the pious hope which I have above expressed, that God's Providence will preserve all such decisions from error.

The last Essay is partly occupied with elucidating my statements about Galileo; and partly with considering a different objection altogether. It has been suggested to me by one or two friends, that this objection requires a more prolonged and careful reply than I had given. I proceed, therefore, to make such reply.

Here is the objection, as stated in my Essay (p. 191). "Ultramontane controversialists constantly assert that no Papal declaration is ex cathedrâ, unless it expresses or implies an *anathema* on the tenet which it condemns. The strongest Ultramontanes, then, do not consider the Pope to speak as Universal Teacher, when he pronounces a lower censure than that of *heresy*."

Now, I am quite confident myself, that these writers intended to say exactly what I have expressed in pp. 192-4.

Another meaning, however, may imaginably be ascribed to them; viz., that the Pope, *speaking by himself*, is not infallible, except in condemning a tenet as *heretical;* but that the *Pope and bishops jointly* possess a further infallibility, viz., in pronouncing *minor censures*. I never heard, indeed, of such an opinion: but if any inquirer is disposed to it, he will find nothing in the present volume to interfere with his conclusion; for (as I have said) I have addressed myself exclusively, not to the "subject," but the "object" of infallibility. Nor, again, would it be worth while, I think, to take any pains to refute it; because in these days the Episcopate invariably accepts and confirms all Papal teaching.

But the present objector ascribes to the large body of theologians a view fundamentally different from either of these: he considers them to teach, that the whole Ecclesia Docens is fallible—and not *in*fallible—in pronouncing censures below that of heresy. I must maintain in reply, that there is no one fact in Theology more absolutely certain, than the contradictory of this statement. My direct and peremptory proof is this: There are several Pontifical declarations—as the censure of Luther, of Baius, of Molinos, of Quesnel—in which the Pope condemns a number of propositions—some as heretical and others as unsound in a lesser degree—without specifying at all which censure appertains to which proposition. Moreover, all the Pontifical declarations above cited have been accepted by the Episcopate. Now, it is at once evident, that there is no one proposition in this whole mass, of which we can know that it was condemned precisely as heretical. And consequently—if that view were true which the objector ascribes to the most eminent theologians—there is no one proposition in the whole mass, of which we can know that it is *infallibly* condemned at all. Now, without here saying more of Luther and of Molinos, the Bulls against Baius and Quesnel are among the most prominent and momentous in all modern theology; and every author carefully refers to them. I ask the objector to point out, if he can, one single approved theologian, who has so much as hinted the faintest doubt that the tenets of

Baius and of Quesnel have been infallibly condemned. And yet, if the objection were well founded to which I am now replying, not one theologian only, but the whole body of theologians, would deny this infallibility altogether. They would hold, indeed, that those propositions, which have been pronounced *heretical*, infallibly deserve that sentence; but they must also admit, that we have no means whatever of knowing what those particular propositions are.

I cannot, of course, within due bounds, adduce quotations, in support of my remark, from all the approved theologians of the Church. For more than one reason, therefore, I will choose as my representative instance the well-known and admirable Theology of the Würtemberg Jesuits. And it is important to show, at starting, that no writers can be more express than they are, in using that language, concerning the Pope's infallibility, on which the whole objection before us rests as on its basis. "The Pope," they say, "is considered as Universal Teacher, when, using his public authority as the Church's supreme guide (magister), he proposes something to the whole Church, obliging all the faithful, *under anathema or pain of heresy*, to believe the thing so proposed with internal assent and Divine faith" (De Principiis Theologicis, n. 190). Now, look at the language of these same theologians, and the facts adduced by them, in reference to Quesnel's condemnation,

The Bull "Unigenitus" is . . . *a dogmatical definition, properly so called.* The reason is, that *it has all the conditions required for a dogmatic judgment.* For (1.) it proposes something to be proscribed, . . . and something also *to be believed;* viz., that there is no one of the condemned propositions, which does not deserve some one, at least, of those *notes of censure* which are expressed in the Bull. . . . (2.) It pronounces *a universal judgment directed to all.* . . . (3.) It has for its object not words, but dogma and doctrine. . . . (4.) It was enacted by a legitimate superior, viz., the Supreme Pontiff, and in due method. . . . (5.) It obtained the Church's consent; since it was acknowledged and proclaimed *as a dogmatical definition* by all the Supreme Pontiffs who followed Clement XI.; by the Synods of Rome, of Avignon, and of Embrun, held on that very matter; by the French bishops, in various assemblies and pastorals; . . . by the metropolitans of the Catholic world, with the express or tacit consent of their suffragans.

The Bull "Unigenitus" does not fail in its character of dogmatic definition, from the circumstance that the censures against Quesnel's propositions were pronounced "in globo" [*i.e.* without any specification which censure is intended for which proposition], . . . because it is *made manifest* (constat) by such a censure that *all the propositions are to be rejected* ("De Gratiâ," n. 243, 244).

This is very unmistakable; but observe carefully what next follows. An objection is raised, precisely the same with that which I have been considering; see how these theologians reply:—

First Objection: "A dogmatic judgment or rule of faith should propose to the faithful dogmata and articles of faith, whereto all men are bound to assent, *under pain of anathema.* But the Bull 'Unigenitus' *does not propose articles of faith,* nor impose an obligation of assenting *under anathema or note of heresy;* therefore it is not a dogmatic judgment or *Rule of Faith.*"

We answer (1). "A Rule of Faith, *strictly so called,* should propose articles of faith," we agree. "A Rule of Faith *in a less strict sense,*" we deny.

We answer (2). This Rule of Faith in a less strict sense—though the Church is *free from all error* [in putting it forth], *because of the*

Holy Ghost's infallible assistance—yet contains within the sphere of its object any truth whatsoever (veritatem quamcunque), although it may not have been [directly] pronounced by God; to which [truth], *although sincere assent of mind and heart be due*, yet the assent *of faith* is *not* due. . . . Hence, he who rejects it is called disobedient, rebellious, or schismatical; but not a heretic. . . .

From these things we infer, that the Bull "Unigenitus" is not a Rule of Faith *in the strict sense*; yet it is *a dogmatical judgment which serves to direct the faithful in the order of faith*: as was pronounced by *the cardinals, archbishops, and bishops assembled at Paris in* 1728, concerning those *judgments of the Church* which contain only respective qualifications (n. 245).

In the discussion which follows, the Würtemberg theologians use incidentally the following expressions:—

These censures "in globo" have this in them fixed and determined, that the Church wills us *to be certain* (velit nos certos fieri)—that the propositions which she condemns *are to be rejected*, as being respectively heretical, erroneous, scandalous; and *to this is referred the assent due to authority*.

It is certain that by force of the Bull the faithful are only commanded not to *think*, teach, or preach otherwise than is contained in the Bull . . . that the implied precept is satisfied by *judging interiorly* that all the propositions are justly condemned.

Let us now look at a very few of the facts, adduced by these theologians in support of their view. We will not here quote the dicta of Popes, because these are well known to all; but only of councils and of other bishops. The Council of Embrun:—

"The constitution 'Unigenitus' . . . is the *dogmatic, definitive, and irretractable* judgment of that Church, concerning which it was said by God, 'the gates of Hell shall not prevail against her.' If any one, therefore, does not assent (acquiescit) to that constitution *in heart and mind* . . . let him be accounted *among those who have made shipwreck concerning the Faith*."

The Würtemberg theologians further state these facts :—

The Catholic metropolitans throughout the world declared expressly, that they and their suffragans held the Constitution as a right and holy law, to which all the faithful are *bound* to render *full submission of mind* (n. 241).

Cardinal Noailles [who had originally praised Quesnel's book], said in a Pastoral : "I admonish all the faithful who are of my diocese that it is in no respect lawful to *think* the contrary of the things which have been defined by the aforesaid Constitution" (n. 246).

On this particular argument—which of itself must be admitted as absolutely final and conclusive — it cannot be necessary to speak further. But I will add two or three, among the multitude of corroborations which throng on my mind. In my Essay I observe : "We believe that in every single instance a careful study of the writer's argument will show clearly the soundness of our interpretation." Let me expand this a little. For what purpose does an Ultramontane controversialist put forth that limitation of Papal infallibility, on which the whole objection is based? To prevent Gallicans and Protestants from citing against him irrelevant instances. "This, that, or the other Pope made a doctrinal mistake," say Gallicans. "Yes, but did he teach that mistake ex cathedrâ?" inquires their opponent. "The mistake you cite," he adds, "was a private and personal mistake; and we never alleged that Popes are divinely guaranteed against private and personal mistakes." Now, I ask this. Do Ultramontane controversialists ever admit that any Pope has made a mistake *in a public and authoritative condemnation, published by him, of some tenet?* And do they add that such admission is consistent with Ultramontane doctrine, because the mistake occurs, not in condemning a tenet as *heretical*, but in pronouncing some lower censure? If no Ultramontane controversialist ever admits this in any one given case, what can be more unreasonable than to suppose, that he intends at starting to admit it as a general principle?

Then, again, take any one you please of the Bulls issued respectively against Luther, Baius, Molinos, Quesnel: see how strange a contradiction is involved in the objector's view. According to him, the Pope speaks ex cathedrâ always, and only, when he condemns a tenet as *heretical.* Since, therefore, in the case before us, the Pope condemns certain tenets as heretical, *some* part of his pronouncement is ex cathedrâ. But there is no single tenet which can be named, of which you can say that it has been condemned by him as heretical; consequently, *no* part of the pronouncement is ex cathedrâ.

Next let us dwell on Fénélon's case. His condemnation did not ascribe to him heresy, directly or indirectly; and, consequently, if the Church's infallibility does not extend beyond her condemnation of heresy, he was not condemned infallibly at all. Now (1.) what was Fénélon's own language? "The bishops of the province," he said to them, "although natural judges of doctrine,—in the present assembly and under present circumstances, cannot pronounce any judgment, except one of simple adhesion to that of the Holy See and acceptance of its Constitution." * Fénélon, be it remembered, was a faithful Ultramontane, in France the head-quarters of Gallicanism; and every one will see that he is here, of set purpose, vigorously expressing his Ultramontanism. In other words, he is declaring that the Pope's Constitution is infallible, independently of episcopal concurrence; and that the bishops had no right of delivering any judgment on the matter, except that of adhesion to the Holy See. Fénélon then, at all events, did not dream of confining Papal infallibility to actual definitions of faith.

(2.) Neither did the French bishops dream of so confining *the Church's* infallibility, though, of course, they denied the Pope's. See the note in p. 193 of this volume. In other words, the question between Ultramontanes and Gallicans referred wholly to the "subject" of infallibility; and with both sides it was an admitted principle, that the same authority which is infallible in condemning tenets as heretical, is no less infallible in pronouncing on them some inferior censure.

(3.) Fénélon, beyond all possible question, accepted his condemnation as infallibly just; and he has been praised universally, throughout the Catholic world, for

* Quoted by De Maistre (du Pape, book i, c. 16), in a note.

his prompt and profound submission. Cardinal Pacca (see p. 56 of this volume), by Gregory XVI.'s desire, held his conduct up to Lamennais for imitation. But had the Church's judgment not been really infallible, such unreserved submission would have been, not laudable, but reprehensible. No one, indeed, will doubt, that the whole Catholic world from that day to this has treated the condemnation as infallible. The whole Catholic world then regards the Church as infallible in her pronouncement of minor censures.

These replies to the objector, added to those contained in my Essay, will (I hope) be considered to suffice. But many more are in reserve, if wanted.

I will now add a few miscellaneous remarks in conclusion. It will be evident, that I have argued throughout exclusively as addressing Catholics; and that I have simply professed to investigate the Church's teaching, on the matter in hand. In case non-Catholics should argue against my thesis, whether on historical grounds or otherwise, I may not impossibly take an opportunity of replying; but nothing of the kind must be expected in the following pages. Of course I hold, without the shadow of a doubt, that no historical argument can really disprove my thesis; just as I hold, without the shadow of a doubt, that no historical argument can really disprove the Divine Institution of Papal Supremacy, or the Divine Revelation of the Trinity. In all these cases alike I hold this without the shadow of a doubt: not because, in any one of the three instances, I have personally examined every imaginable historical difficulty; but because I know for certain that the Church's teaching is infallibly true.

More than one of the articles, from which these Essays are taken, contained some severe criticisms on particular writers. No part of my work in carrying on the *Dublin Review* is so trying and distasteful to me, as my personal conflict with individuals; nor have I ever entered on such a conflict otherwise than with extreme reluctance, and in obedience to what I thought a plain duty. No such considerations of duty, however, oblige me to reprint any of these personal criticisms; and it is a great relief to me, therefore, that I can omit them altogether.

It has been said by some of my readers, that I have shown repulsive arrogance, by the confident tone in which I have expressed my convictions. Now, far be it from me to deny, that arrogance and a hundred other faults enter largely into my moral composition; and I shall be unfeignedly grateful to those, who see in my writing manifold traces of those faults, if they will pray for my improvement. Never, certainly, was a good cause supported by a more unworthy advocate. But I really cannot admit that the confidence of my tone has been in itself a proof of arrogance. I have been confident in maintaining my main theses, because it seems to me so absolutely unquestionable, by any one who takes pains to examine, that the Church teaches them. But the outline traced by the Church has to be filled up with various particulars and in various details; as will be seen *e. g.* in pp. 50, 51: and in regard to these particulars and details, I do not think any reader will say that I have expressed myself with undue confidence.

Indeed, the very principles which I advocate afford, I hope, much security against undue intellectual self-confidence. In conformity with those principles, every single proposition contained in this volume, which bears ever so remotely on faith and morals—and there is hardly a sentence which has not such a bearing—is submitted by me with most absolute unreserve to the infallible judgment of the Holy See. Take any statement which may have been made by me with the greatest confidence: if the Holy Father shall see reason to censure it, my conviction of its unsoundness will be (not merely far greater in degree, but) indefinitely higher in kind, than my present persuasion of its truth.

LONDON, *January* 20, 1866.

CONTENTS.

ESSAY I.

On Theological Errors below that of Heresy.

ESSAY II.

The Pope's Declaration on his Civil Princedom.

ESSAY III.

Infallibility Claimed for the Encyclical "Mirari vos."

ESSAY IV.

Infallibility Claimed for the Recent Encyclical and Syllabus.

ESSAY V.

The Church Infallible in her Magisterium.

ESSAY VI.

ESSAY VII.

Doctrinal Decrees of a Pontifical Congregation.

ESSAY VIII.

The Case of Galileo.

ESSAY IX.

Reply to Two Objections.

ESSAY I.*

ON THEOLOGICAL ERRORS BELOW HERESY.

WE have hitherto been arguing on the supposition, that the Munich Brief is in no sense infallible. But we are now to maintain, as we have already expressed ourselves, that though it neither is nor professes to be a strict definition of faith, its theological declarations are nevertheless infallibly true. This assertion we consider to be indubitable, no less on Gallican than on Ultramontane grounds, so soon as we have had time for full certainty that the Catholic Episcopate assents to the Pontifical judgment. For the sake, however, of brevity and clearness, we will express ourselves throughout in accordance with that Ultramontane principle, which is not only held by the vast majority of theologians, but of which we are convinced that it is the one true Catholic doctrine. Nothing will be easier, than for those of the other school to adjust our language to the requirements

* July, 1864.—From an Article called "Rome and the Munich Congress," pp. 79—96.

of their theory. All this portion of our argument, indeed, will be expressed in the merest skeleton form and outline; for to illustrate and expand it would be to write a good-sized theological volume. And it will be seen as we proceed, that our argument tends, not only to vindicate that right which the Brief undoubtedly possesses, of being humbly and dutifully accepted on the ground of authority; but that it serves other purposes also. It will be found to give us the greatest possible advantage, in appreciating the practical result of those errors which the Brief condemns; and it is also available (though this is beyond the scope of our present article) for the purpose of theologically defending the whole doctrine of the Brief. First, then, for the foundation of our argument.

No error was ever broached more obviously absurd, than that the assent of divine faith is due to no other doctrines, except those which the Church has expressly defined. Many other errors, perhaps, have been equally pernicious with this, but hardly any, surely, can have been so obviously ridiculous. Every one mentions it as one extraordinary peculiarity attending the definition of the Immaculate Conception, that such definition was not required by any existing misbelief; while as to the Church's earliest definitions, it is quite proverbial that they were invariably put forth "propter insurgentes hæreses." To say, therefore, that the Church taught no doctrines as of faith before she defined them, is to say that before heresies arose she had no faith at all. Can anything, indeed, be more extravagant than to imagine, that before Arius's condemnation, there was no heresy in thinking that the Son of God had a beginning of existence? or that before the condemnation of Apollonaris, there was no heresy in denying to Him a human soul? or that before Luther's condemnation, there was no heresy in thinking the faith required for justification to be a man's firm belief in his own acceptance and certainty of salvation? All those doctrines are in every age portions of the Catholic Faith, and to disbelieve or doubt them is heresy, which (as the Munich Brief expresses it) "are delivered [to the faithful] as divinely revealed by the ordinary teaching of the whole Church dispersed throughout the world."

Moreover, these doctrines may be thus delivered either (1) "expressly" or (2) "practically;"—*i. e.* (1) by direct statement, or (2) by obvious and immediate implication. Thus, in teaching my child the "Our Father," I "practically" teach him that it is his duty to forgive them that trespass against him.* The number of truths thus practically taught by the Church is very considerable, as a little thought will convince us. Thus, from the first, in prescribing penitential exercises, she has practically taught that such exercises are acceptable to God; in inculcating prayers for the dead, she has practically taught that they may be benefited by prayer; in baptizing children, she has practically taught (what many Protestants have since

---

* It might seem more obvious, rather to use the words "explicitly" and "implicitly," than "directly" and "practically." But according to theological usage, a doctrine is said to be taught "implicitly" by the Church, if she teaches some other doctrines from which it is a logical deduction. Now a doctrine which the Church teaches "implicitly" only in this sense, is *not* taught by her as an integral portion of the Catholic Faith. She may *afterwards*, indeed, "explicitly" teach it; but that is a different question.

denied) that the administration of sacraments to unconscious recipients is not necessarily against Christ's institution; in her various Eucharistic ceremonies, she has practically taught that some great and august mystery is there contained. Indeed, generally, prayers, religious ceremonies, pious usages, each has its own obvious and immediate doctrinal implication; and with the mass of men it is far more by such means as these than by direct statement, that Catholic dogma sinks deeply, though silently, into the heart, seizes the convictions, and influences the will.*

What, then, is the origin, and what the advantage, of doctrinal definitions? Their first origin, as has been already said, is ordinarily the springing up of some heresy. If we look at the Early Church, we shall find that, so soon as this takes place, the great majority of Catholics recognise its true character, and recoil from it with horror and anathema; while a cer-

---

* Among a thousand instances of the stress laid by theologians on the Church's practical teaching, may be cited two which occur within ten pages of each other in Perrone's "Prælections." In order to prove the Church's teaching on the necessity of Baptism to salvation, he thus argues:—"But *the sense*, both of the Eastern and Western Church, cannot be better inferred, than *from the perpetual solicitude* of baptizing all those who were in danger of death, omitting all solemnities, by the hand of men or women, Catholic, heretical, or infidel." On Baptism, *n.* 139. The other instance is this. Caietan and a few other theologians have thought that the infant children of Catholics, dying unbaptised, may be saved through the faith and prayer of their parents. But, argues Perrone, "If the Church *judged this opinion grounded* (probabilem), she would exhort parents to pray, or elicit the act of faith, in order that their unborn children might be saved; which, however, *she has never done.*" *n.* 156.

tain minority are deceived by the heresiarch's sophistry, and think that his tenets do not so very widely diverge from what has hitherto been taught. It becomes, then, the office of the Ecclesia Docens (1) to anathematize the heresy; and (2) to give some intellectual analysis of the assailed doctrine, which shall be sufficiently clear and precise for marking out intelligibly and distinctly its points of contrast with the insurgent error. Here already are two different advantages accruing from definitions: (1) they make Catholics quite certain that this or that doctrine is of faith, whereas it was previously possible that opinions might differ on this head; and (2) they give a certain intellectual analysis of the doctrine in question.

But further, the attention of Catholics is now specially called to this particular doctrine, and they occupy themselves with pious zeal in its further intellectual analysis; and thus the science of theology has its beginning. The Church has ever encouraged this habit of intellectual analysis; which performs for her the highest services, in preserving and deepening the uniformity of religious belief; and which, indeed, is but one part of that general exercise of reason on revealed principles, which she has ever most warmly promoted. On the other hand, in order that those services may be truly performed, in order that the Catholic's exercise of reason may tend to edification and not to gradual subversion of dogma, her supervision over the whole progress of theological science must be vigilant and minute. Such supervision she has ever exercised; and she so prizes the theological science which has thus grown up under her fostering care, that not only does she earnestly recommend its study as the authoritative exposition and illustration of her creed, but erects various of its enunciations into infallible decrees of faith. This takes place in more than one way. Thus that precise cycle of doctrines, which she has expressly or practically taught as of faith from the first, may be proposed by her, as time advances, in a deeper, fuller, clearer theological analysis. Again, a doctrine may be defined, which has not hitherto been taught (either expressly or practically) as an integral part of the Catholic Faith; but in regard to which, intellectual investigation has clearly established that it was taught by the Apostles or is contained in Scripture. Or a controversy may have arisen, whether some doctrine were in fact revealed originally by God; and this controversy she may infallibly determine. And thus there comes to exist extensively a second class of definitions. Those which we first mentioned do but declare some doctrine to be of faith which Catholics were obliged to believe as of faith before the definition was issued; but those of which we have been last speaking, impose on Catholics an obligation which did not before exist; as in the most remarkable instance of the Immaculate Conception.*

These foundations having been briefly laid, we proceed with equal brevity to build on them our argument.

1. It is the duty of the Ecclesia Docens, not merely to preserve the deposit of faith pure at any given period, but to watch jealously against the entrance into Catholic thought of any dangerous element, which may *hereafter* be injurious to such purity. Suppose,

* Perrone draws a distinction between these two different classes of definitions: *De Locis Theologicis*, pars 3, n. 339.

e. g., some proposition begins to find acceptance with certain Catholics, which by necessary consequence would lead to heresy; though these Catholics themselves have not pursued it into that consequence: she cannot fulfil her trust, unless she peremptorily banish that proposition from Catholic thought. But it is plain that she cannot possibly effect this, unless she have the power of infallibly declaring that it *is* an error; no such interior assent, as can reasonably be given to a fallible declaration, would commonly suffice for the sure expulsion of such error from the whole body of Catholic thinkers. The same argument applies with equal force to other propositions, which may not indeed lead by *legitimate consequence* to heresy, but which are yet so connected with it in fact, that, unless effectually expelled, they will certainly introduce it. Hence the Ecclesia Docens has the gift of pronouncing infallibly, not merely that such a proposition is heretical, but that such another is theologically unsound, though not heretical. If she had not this gift, she would have no means of preventing the gradual (and perhaps speedy) inroads of heresy among her flock; and so could not faithfully preserve the Deposit committed to her charge.

2. If the Ecclesia Docens certainly and evidently possesses this power, it must in itself be mortally sinful to hold, that a proposition which she censures does not deserve the censure affixed to it; though we are by no means saying that the mortal sin is one of heresy. We should only add, that since even in the case of defined doctrines invincible ignorance is universally admitted as an excuse for unbelief, much more in such cases as these.

3. In order that a doctrine may be of faith, it is not necessary (as we have seen) that the Ecclesia Docens should expressly define it: it suffices if she expressly or practically teaches it throughout her territory, as revealed by God. In like manner, if I could know for certain that the Ecclesia Docens throughout her whole territory, with full cognizance and sanction of the Holy See, expressly or practically teaches the unsoundness of a certain proposition, I should know with precisely equal certainty that such proposition *is* unsound. And it would in itself be a mortal sin, if, possessing such knowledge, I dared to embrace the proposition as true or doubt its falsehood. But, where the Church has not expressly spoken, is there any means by which I can *become* thus absolutely certain that the Ecclesia Docens practically condemns the proposition? Perhaps the attainment of absolute certainty is not often possible; but take such a case as this. Suppose some question to have been actively ventilated by theologians; and the whole body of them without exception to have come confidently to the conclusion, that certain propositions relating to it are theologically unsound. Suppose also the Holy Father and the whole Ecclesia Docens to be well acquainted with this fact, and to display no kind of disapprobation, but rather the contrary. A moral certainty would thence arise that she practically teaches the unsoundness of such propositions; and a consequent obligation to abstain from all assent to them.*

* So much sanction as this, *e. g.*, may undoubtedly be claimed for a certain body of doctrine on the endowments of our Lord's Sacred Humanity, which is maintained by all theologians; which is taken for granted in all books of meditation and spiritual reading, wherever the subject is mentioned; and which is especially dear to devout Catholics.

4. Just as various propositions may be theologically unsound on the subject of the Trinity, or of Grace, so also on the subject of the Church. Take, for instance, the theses condemned in this Munich Brief. It is quite *imaginable* that these propositions are theologically unsound; or, in other words, that even if not heretical, they tend directly in one way or an other to impugnment of some particular contained in that doctrine respecting the Church which was revealed by Christ.

5. That power which the Catholic Episcopate can exercise collectively, the Holy Father can exercise individually, as the Church's ruler. That infallibility which the Catholic Episcopate possesses collectively, the Holy Father possesses individually, as the Church's teacher. Here it is that we part company with Gallican opinions; but our proposition is held by the large majority of Catholic theologians.

Now let us apply these various principles to this case of the Munich Brief. In the first place, we can see no kind of reason for doubting that its doctrinal declarations are put forth by the Holy Father in his capacity of Universal Teacher, and are therefore in themselves infallible. The supposed objector, to whom we referred at starting, raises two difficulties in the way of this conclusion: (1) the Brief is not formally addressed to the Universal Church, but to the Archbishop of Munich; and (2) it does not express or imply an ascription of heresy to the various theses which it opposes. We will take these two difficulties in order.

When the Holy Father has put forth any exposition of doctrine, inquiry is made whether he does so as

Universal Teacher or merely as a private doctor.* One test given, to make us certain of the former alternative, is its being addressed formally to the Universal Church. But we are here certain of this alternative on grounds altogether distinct. For the Brief professes on its surface to have been elicited by that anxiety for the pure preservation of dogma, which Pius IX. experiences as occupying "this Apostolic See;" as having "committed to him by Christ the Lord, the most grave duty of ruling and governing His whole Church, and feeding all His flock with the pastures of salutary doctrine, and constantly watching that the most holy faith and its teaching (*ejusque doctrina*) may never suffer any detriment."

And our argument is greatly illustrated by the Brief of 1859, which condemned Gunther. This also was addressed to an individual pastor, the Archbishop of Cologne; yet no one has ever doubted that the Pope issued it as Universal Teacher, and that he condemned Gunther in that capacity. Indeed, in a later Brief of 1860, he states, as a "reductio ad absurdum" of some proposition which he censures, that to uphold it would be to imply that his condemnation of Gunther had

* Some few theologians (with whom, however, we cannot agree) suggest a third alternative—viz., that he may publish a doctrinal decision, not as Universal Teacher, nor yet as a private doctor; but as the head of some Congregation. In the present instance, at all events, there is no need for considering this alternative, as there is no intervention of any Congregation in the matter The case of his sanctioning some doctrinal decision, though he does not himseif publish it, will be considered in the article on Galileo.

been erroneous.* It is quite certain, then, that though that Brief was addressed to an individual, the Pope issued it as Universal Teacher, and claimed to be infallible in its decisions. There is a certain difference, no doubt, between the two letters addressed respectively to the Archbishops of Cologne and of Munich: in the former the Pope speaks expressly of certain errors having been promulgated; in the latter, he carefully abstains from doing so. But a moment's consideration will show, that this difference in no way affects the dogmatic authority of the Munich Brief. For the Holy Father exhibits no reserve whatever, in condemning most stringently the errors against which he inveighs; his only reserve concerns the question of *fact*, whether such fundamental errors can really have been advocated in an assembly of Catholic theologians.

The second difficulty raised has no greater force than the first. It is true (no doubt) that the Pope in no part of this Brief ascribes *heresy* to the censured errors; and this (no doubt also) would suffice to show that it is not a definition of faith. But no one ever thought it was; we only maintain that it is an infallible condemnation of certain theses, not necessarily as heretical, but as theologically unsound in one or other degree. And certain though it is that he does not impute to them heresy, it is equally certain that he does impute to them theological unsoundness. This

* "Ad quod si Baltzer animum advertisset, intellexisset sanè doctrinam de homine quam in suo scripto profitetur, tanquam ecclesiasticis dogmatibus consentaneam, defendere, idem esset atque nosmet incusare quòd in Guntherianâ doctrinâ judicandâ erraverimus."

is evident in his censure of the attacks directed against scholastic theology. Here, again, is another passage of the Brief, and a truly momentous one :—

> Even though the question concerned that subjection [of the intellect] which is to be yielded in an act of divine faith, yet that would have not to be confined to those things which have been hitherto defined by the express decrees of Œcumenical Councils or of Roman Pontiffs and this Apostolic See, but to be extended to those things also which are delivered [to the faithful] as divinely revealed by the ordinary authority [magisterium] of the whole Church dispersed throughout the world, and are therefore accounted by Catholic theologians, with universal and consistent consent, to appertain to the faith. But since the question concerns that subjection by which all those Catholics are bound in conscience who apply themselves to the speculative sciences, in order that by their writings they may confer new benefits on the Church, therefore the men of the above-named Congress should recognize that it is not sufficient for learned [sapientibus] Catholics to receive and revere the before-mentioned dogmas of the Church; but that is also necessary (*opus esse*) for them to subject themselves, as well to the doctrinal decisions which are issued by the Pontifical Congregations, as also to those heads of doctrine which are retained by the common and consistent consent of Catholics as theological truths, and as conclusions so certain, that opinions adverse to the same, though they cannot be called heretical, yet deserve some other theological censure. Therefore we do not think that the men who were present at the above-mentioned Congress of Munich either could or would have opposed *the doctrine now expounded* [nunc expositæ] which is retained in the Church [as flowing] *from the principles of true theology.*

The Holy Father thus expresses a distinct judgment, that to "oppose the doctrine here expounded," is to oppose "the principles of true theology;" or (in other words) is theologically unsound. And when the supposed objector takes for granted that the Pope only speaks ex cathedrâ when he condemns heresy, and not also when he condemns theological error of any kind, we may at least call on him for some proof of so gratuitous and anti-Catholic an opinion. *

We are to show, lastly, the real drift and tendency of those errors, which the Holy Father has now condemned; and at starting we observe a very important distinction, which marks them off from Frohschammer's errors, condemned in 1862. Each of the two erroneous systems, indeed, seeks to obtain for secular science a far more complete emancipation from ecclesiastical authority, than sound doctrine permits. But they aim at their common end by different methods: the earlier system by trying unduly to emancipate secular science from the control of theological, the latter by trying unduly to emancipate theological science from the control of ecclesiastical authority. And thus the phenomenon has originated, to which attention has often been drawn; viz., that although the direct theme of this Munich Brief is the due subordination of secular science, yet the errors which it mainly condemns are most strictly within the sphere of theology. In order, however, to understand exactly the state of the case, we must begin with a few prefatory remarks on the relation between religion and secular science.

Theological science, we need hardly say, is generated by the exercise of reason on principles known by revelation; secular science, in its various branches, by the exercise of reason on principles known by reason itself, or by experience. Religion, however, and secular science are constantly crossing each other; and very many are the truths which belong equally to both.

---

* One argument, which has been sometimes attempted for this opinion, will be noticed in the Appendix to the article on Galileo.

This happens in more ways than one. Firstly, the doctrinal Deposit committed to the Church's keeping has the closest relation with philosophy; it possesses no one constituent, which may not be assailed on strictly philosophical grounds. A large portion, indeed, of Catholic dogma is in its own nature within the sphere of reason; though, of course, it is a very different question, how far unassisted reason would have advanced in its exploration. The Church's whole moral doctrine, for example, is so circumstanced, and her whole exposition of God's Attributes. But doctrine the most purely supernatural may easily come into contact with (erroneous) philosophy. Thus, the Church's teaching on Grace may be indefinitely corrupted and falsified by unsound psychology; nay, even such mysteries as the Trinity, the Incarnation, Transubstantiation, may be opposed by a chain of philosophical reasoning, purporting to show that they are intrinsically impossible. Here, then, is one way, in which religion and secular science may easily be brought into conflict. Another way is by means of the various facts, which are either inseparably mixed up with the very foundations of Christianity, or else are stated in that Inspired Volume which the Church authenticates; for both these classes of facts may easily be in apparent collision with the conclusions whether of historical or of physical science. We see, therefore, over how vast a field of secular science the Church's authority extends. She has the power (as we have pointed out) of infallibly pronouncing propositions to be erroneous, if they tend by legitimate consequence to a denial of any religious doctrine which she teaches. But secular science contains a vast number of such propositious; and on all these, therefore, the Church has power to pronounce an infallible judgment.

We may here notice, by the way, a transparently fallacious argument, which has occasionally been used by Catholic writers of the school which we are criticising. Such writers sometimes speak, as though nothing were further from their wish than to meddle with theology itself. Their aim, it seems, is merely to introduce some more satisfactory harmony between religion and secular science, than has hitherto prevailed; and they complain that the Church should look with a jealous eye on what (as they think) appertains so very indirectly to her province. A transparent fallacy indeed! Their allegation assumes, as a matter of fact, that certain propositions, generally accounted as true conclusions of theological science, are in conflict with certain other propositions, which are generally accounted as true conclusions of this or that secular science. If this fact be granted them, it follows that two different methods are imaginable of removing such apparent conflict between the sciences: firstly, by showing that the former propositions are not true conclusions of theological science; and, secondly, by showing that the latter are not true conclusions of secular science. If these writers adopt the latter method, there is no pretence for saying that the Church has ever shown the slightest disposition to interfere with them in any way whatever. But if they adopt the former, they are simply treading on theological ground; and they are absolutely under the Church's jurisdiction, as though they were writing formal treatises on the Trinity or the Incarnation.

What, then, is the true spirit, what the proper attitude towards the Church, in which theological investigations should be pursued? The Church, as we have seen, practically teaches an indefinite number of doctrines as integral parts of the Catholic Faith, which she has not expressly defined; and her infallibility, moreover, extends to a large cycle of further truths, which are not in themselves integral parts of the Catholic Faith at all. In the following truly admirable passage, the Bishop of Birmingham has most forcibly expressed the same general truth:—

Unquestionably there is what I may call an outer and an inner theology, a variable and a fixed element in that loftiest of sciences. Yet they run so into each other, that it is impossible to treat them like separate bodies, or practically to class them in distinct compartments. There is a theology, the conclusions of which rest so completely on revealed premises that they cannot be separated from Faith. And there are other conclusions elicited from revealed propositions by the direct appliance of fundamental certainties in the natural order, which therefore present a most certain and unanimous theology, or what is equivalent to it. *Many things go to form the integral belief of the Church that were never formally defined; for there is an unwritten as there is a written rule of faith, a statute and a common law of believing. The decrees of faith but incorporate and fix the common belief in formal terms, as circumstances call for dogmatic declarations.* The Church treats not her decisions as the Anglican authorities treat their Articles, straining to reduce them to their minimum of sense, in order to accommodate them to a society devoured with unbelief. *Her decisions live in the habits of the faithful, and express not more but less than her entire belief.* They are sustained and environed by a yet larger and more comprehensive tradition; they are expanded by the theologian, and by the preacher, and by the pious meditations and practices both of clergy and laity. They come out of the fulness of that common and unwritten tradition, as well as from the deposit of Holy Scripture; and *there yet remain unfixed by degrees, both doctrines of faith, and dogmatic facts, and moral laws, and* *fundamental principles of the Church's constitution and discipline, without which the Church would not be what Christ has made her.* Under whatever pretext of science or of criticism, and under whatever plea of their not being defined, to attempt to strip religion of these doctrines, or of that inner theology which is inseparable from faith, or from fixed principles such as faith presupposes, or even from the theology generally taught and preached; or to separate religion from that sacred history on which her evidence, her doctrine, or her edification reposes; would be to incur the charge and the sin of inculcating, as the case may happen to be, heresy, or what approximates to heresy, or is rash, or scandalous, or offensive to pious ears (pp. 55, 56).*

This passage contains some exposition of that most fundamental and pervasive principle, which theologians call "Ecclesiæ juge magisterium;" and a theologian imbued with that principle, throughout his investigations, ever gazes (if we may so speak) on the aspect and countenance of his mother the Church. He is eagerly desirous, that her spirit may be infused into his whole body of thought; that he may understand her decrees according to her true mind; and that he may duly grasp those other doctrines, which she practically teaches without express decree. Every fresh conclusion at which he seems to arrive he distrusts, until he has carefully considered how far it harmonizes with her practical conduct and maxims. And even though each individual conclusion so harmonizes, he is still dissatisfied, unless his whole assemblage of conclusions, his whole *corpus* of doctrine, seems according to her mind, in the respective proportions and emphasis of

---

* *On certain Methods of the "Rambler" and the "Home and Foreign Review."* A Second Letter to the Clergy of the Diocese of Birmingham. By the Right Rev. Bishop Ullathorne.

its various parts. Nay, a good Catholic, even when pursuing secular science on its own ground, will never lose sight of revealed truth, nor of those various living authorities by whose unceasing pronouncements it is infallibly taught. "For although," says the Holy Father, in this Munich Brief, "those natural sciences (disciplinæ) rest on their own proper principles known by reason, yet their Catholic cultivators must have Divine Revelation before them as a directing star, through whose guiding light (quâ prælucente) they may beware of errors and quicksands, wherever in their investigations and arguments (commentationibus) they perceive that they may be led thereby, *as happens very frequently* (ut sæpissimè accidit), to say what is more or less opposed to the infallible truth of those things which have been revealed by God." *

In contrast with this true theological spirit, let us now contemplate the inevitable result of those maxims which the Munich Brief condemns. They may be thus briefly summed up. "The Ecclesia Docens is not infallible, except as regards her express definitions; and where the Church is not infallible, the declaration of her authorities has no more legitimate force, than is

* Many good Catholics have some difficulty in understanding how the exercise of such a principle as this can be made consistent with the admitted independence of secular science on its own ground. There is no question which at the present day more clamours for a full investigation than this; but it is, of course, far too large to be entered on episodically. Perhaps we may be allowed, without impropriety, to refer for some inadequate notice of it, to a Catholic work published some years ago. See Dr. Ward's "Philosophical Introduction," Preface, pp. xxi.—xxvi.

due to the actual arguments which they adduce." On this view, a theologian has simply to take for his principles the definitions (as contained, *e. g.*, in Denzinger's small volume) which have been put forth in various ages by Popes and Councils, and to manipulate them according to his own views of history and logic, with no further deference or submission to the living Church. His private judgment thus exercised may lead him to the opinion, that S. Augustine, whom the Church has ever reverenced as the great doctor of grace, is the virtual founder of a condemned heresy against that very doctrine; or that the scholastic theology is radically unsound, though the Church has not merely cherished it throughout with her warmest favour, but has almost identified herself with it, by incorporating its characteristic thoughts and expressions into her very definitions of faith.* If such are the conclusions in which an inquirer is landed by his private judgment, he will not be deterred, by any reverence for the Church's authority, from holding and even publishing them. In one word, whereas the one fundamental principle of genuine theology is unreserved and eager submission to the "Ecclesiæ juge magisterium," a total refusal of such submission is the one principle pervading this most unsound and poisonous counterfeit. It is, in its whole spirit and bearing, a simple substitution of the Protestant "private judgment" for the Catholic "authority."

So much for theological science in its strictest sense.

* Since this sentence was originally published, we have to thank God for the Church's express condemnation of prop. xiii. in the recent Syllabus.

As to those large portions of secular science which come into contact with theology, writers of this school do not conceal the fact, that they handle them almost entirely in the same way as Protestants; that they handle them with hardly any greater reference to the Church's voice, than if she did not exist. In the number of the *Home and Foreign Review* for January, 1864, we find this remarkable statement:—"Inasmuch as dogmatic utterances [of the Church] are *very rare*, and the [ecclesiastical] authorities which generally intervene in matters of science *have no part in infallibility*, those propositions [adopted at the Munich congress] implicitly claim for science all the freedom which is demanded in Dr. Döllinger's inaugural address" (p. 241). According to these gentlemen, then, Catholics are at liberty to expatiate over the whole domain of secular science—even that part with which theology is most intimately connected—with no submission whatever to any ecclesiastical authority, except to those "dogmatic utterances" which by their own confession are "very rare."

Great is the consolation of remembering, that these shallow, proud, and most pernicious errors are now for ever banished from Catholic theology. But we must not forget, that though these particular errors are put to silence, the spirit which has prompted them still lives in the midst of us. We are far, indeed, from meaning to imply, that this age of the Church is worse than others. Every age in its turn is replete with calamities; and if we read that series of Papal addresses to the Church which we mentioned at an earlier part of our article, we shall see that each successive Pope has regarded his own period as most heavily afflicted.* Whether the evil and irreligiousness of our own time exceed that of others, is a truly unprofitable inquiry; for all times are predominantly evil and irreligious: but what is the particular *kind* of evil and irreligiousness now rampant, is surely of all inquiries the most practical. To us it seems that, among all the Church's heavy afflictions, none is now more grievous than the tendency, not in practice only (as at all times), but even in theory, to separate the general current of thought and action from the influence of religion and of religious teachers. It is, of course, among Protestants that this tendency is far more extensively and formidably exhibited; and the great body of Catholics in these islands seem as yet on the whole (thank God!) faithful to their traditions. But living as they do in habits of constantly increasing familiarity and intimacy with Protestants, it is absurd to doubt that they are in danger of serious harm from the infection of evil principles; and among those lay Catholics who specially profess intellectual culture, the symptoms appear to us truly alarming. Illustrations abound. Sometimes it is implied that clerics and laymen legitimately differ from each other, in their estimate of human life and conduct; nay, it has been

* We think that Pius IX. has hardly issued a single document, which does not contain some reference to the fearful evils by which the Church is now so heavily bowed down. So in the Munich Brief he refers, at starting, to the exceeding bitterness of the time (asperrimis hisce temporibus); and afterwards he speaks of the false opinions which have appeared in Catholic Germany, as adding to the anguish which so many causes contribute to produce. "Hæc sanè omnia . . . . nostrum solicitabant et angebant animum tot aliis pressum angustiis."

called an encroachment on the sacerdotal office, that laymen should address his fellow-Catholics (as at Malines) on the worthlessness of this world's goods. Sometimes it is urged that the moral and religious training of clerics and laymen should differ, not in matters of detail, but in its fundamental principles; a view which, intellectually speaking, is below contempt, unless either it be denied that clerics and laymen have one common nature, or else it be assumed (which *is* really the assumption) that the moral excellence of one class should be measured by a different standard from the moral excellence of the other. Or again, in the various discussions about mixed education, it is often taken for granted that religious instruction and training is but one part out of many; instead of being the one foundation, on which all must be built, under pain of the whole edifice being unsound and rotten. But why dwell on individual questions? Look at the highest spheres of non-ecclesiastical action and speculation respectively, the sphere of politics and the sphere of philosophy. Both these regions are in open and flagrant rebellion against God and the Church. It is held unconsciously by many, and actually expressed by some, that the politician, as such, has no concern with man's supernatural end, and that the philosopher, as such, has no concern with revealed doctrine.* The

* It may, perhaps, be better here to explain. No one pretends that either political action or philosophical speculation is directly under the Church's authority; but both are indirectly under it. The politician, in his political capacity, is bound to defer to the Church, so far as his measures affect the welfare of souls; and the philosopher, in his philosophical capacity, is bound to defer to the Church, so far as his speculations affect revealed doctrine.

Holy See of late has been especially energetic against both these malignant errors. Gregory XVI., in his well-known Encyclical, "Mirari vos," declares authoritatively (in the words of a canonized predecessor), that "the power and authority" of princes is "conferred on them not only for the world's government, but, *most of all*, for the Church's protection." And the present Pope has repeatedly and most earnestly inculcated the obligation incumbent on philosophers and philosophy, of rendering to the Church due submission. It is with very deep truth, then, that an able writer in the *Civiltà* places, in close juxtaposition, two orations delivered almost contemporaneously to Catholic audiences; the one by M. de Montalembert at Malines, the other by Dr. Döllinger at Munich. Both these orations tend to disparage—we need not here determine precisely to how grievous an extent—the Church's legitimate authority, whether in politics or in philosophy.

For ourselves, however, we regard the philosophical movement with immeasurably greater alarm and consternation than the political. No one, indeed, can condemn and repudiate, more unreservedly than we do, M. de Montalembert's whole principle on "the liberty of worships." But, in the first place, a man's view of such matters is almost or altogether apart from his interior life; and even a saintly person, under invincible misapprehension, may hold such opinions. But further, the evil work of de-Catholicizing civil society has been now so completely wrought out in far the largest portion of Europe, that the question at issue rather concerns our theoretical estimate of the past, than our practical provision for the present. It may be said indeed (and truly) that the French orator's principles imply the civil tolerance of such errors, as the religious sense of Europe would still repudiate; of sects, *e. g.*, which might be started on the basis of polygamy or of atheism. But M. de Montalembert is far more given to action than to speculation; and his Catholic instincts would assuredly save him in practice from any such blunder. Indeed, remarkably enough, in his Malines orations, he excepts from his proposed liberality all sects which should deny God's Existence or run counter to natural morality; in other words, he excepts all but those who are tolerated already in far the greatest part of Europe, and with whose external liberty in such regions no Catholic dreams of interfering.

But the other case is widely different. The pursuit of secular science, on the principle of disregard to ecclesiastical decisions, eats like a canker into the whole substance of a man's religion. We have seen that the number of philosophical tenets is enormously large, which lead by legitimate consequence to denial of this or that Catholic verity; what safeguard, then, can be imagined against an inquirer embracing some of these tenets, if he makes it his very principle to disregard those ecclesiastical declarations which condemn them? Here, then, we have to suppose a man engaged in active philosophical speculation, who still believes in Catholicism, but who holds also certain philosophical tenets, which in their result are antagonistic thereto. He has, of course, started on a road, which has no end except apostacy. At what pace he advances along that road, will depend on the degree in which he unites intellectual keenness with spiritual obtuseness; but every day will bring him nearer to his unhappy goal, unless God give him grace to retrace his steps and renounce his fundamental principle. He naturally tries every attainable method to relieve himself from the burden of two contradictory convictions; and so gradually sinks from bad to worse. First, he refuses to believe any Catholic doctrine which is not strictly defined. Next, as to the defined doctrines themselves, he more and more chooses to confine his acceptance of them to the lowest sense which their words will grammatically bear, instead of studying the Church's full intention. Then a current of thought finds outward vent, which has long been silently proceeding; and he both thinks and speaks of the Church's rulers with compassionate contempt. He regards them much as he might regard Balaam's ass: they are made the organs of a divine utterance, he thinks, at certain very wide intervals, but are otherwise below the ordinary level of humanity, in their apprehension of God's works and ways. It is difficult to know how long this state of mind can last; but one would think the time could not be far distant, when he would find himself in a direct opposition to the Church's teaching which no sophistry can gloss over, and be confronted with the awful alternative of total retractation or undisguised apostacy.

It might be said, perhaps, that deplorable as such an exhibition may be, at least but very few are exposed to these awful perils; and that in this respect political liberalism is far more disastrous than philosophical. But, on the contrary, "the instructed minority" exercise an enormous influence on man's destiny; a degree of influence which is not exaggerated, we believe, by the said "instructed minority" themselves. It is not the effect produced by them on their contemporaries which is so formidable, but the effect produced in forming the convictions and maxims of the rising generation. And no doubt it is a sense of this which animates Catholic authorities in the movement now proceeding in so many different parts of Christendom —nowhere more than in Rome itself—for elevating ecclesiastical education in its intellectual aspect. It is this, we are convinced, next to directly spiritual means, in which the true remedy is to be found for evils whose fearfulness and imminence it is difficult to exaggerate. It will be a very great boon also if (as the *Civiltà* article induces us to hope) these controversies may lead to a renewed cultivation of the scholastic theology. We are confident that neither scriptural, nor patristic, nor historical studies, necessary as they are, can produce their due result, unless built on the scientific mastery of dogma. Now, as the *Civiltà* writer most truly remarks, the scholastic cannot be called the *best* scientific theology taught in the Church, simply because she neither teaches nor has ever taught any other. But we are wandering to a theme which would require an article for itself.

The mention, however, of the *Civiltà* leads us to one final consideration, deeper than any which has preceded. "We have learned," says the writer in question very opportunely, "not from the scholastics, but from the Catechism, that the end for which man was placed in the world is to save his soul, and not to construct linguistic science, historical criticism, and biblical exegesis." The certain and unfailing result of intellectual rebellion is practically to forget, some go the length of explicitly denying, this foundation of all; and such a fact not only throws men into direct antagonism with the Church's spirit, but takes from them all power of appreciating (even if they wished it) her maxims and demeanour. It is said (we know not how truly) of Mr. Telford, the eminent engineer, that in his view rivers were created for the one purpose of feeding canals. According to him, then, each individual river is more excellent of its kind, more perfect, more admirable, in proportion as it is better adapted to fulfil this the great end of its existence. If such were really his whim, it would follow, as a matter of course, that whatever judgment he formed on the relative excellence of rivers was simply untrustworthy and ridiculous; in ninety-nine cases out of a hundred it would be absurdly wrong, and if in the hundredth it happened to be approximately right, this circumstance would be due purely to accident. In like manner, if any one goes astray on the first principles of human conduct—if he is at sea as to the very end for which man was created,—every judgment which he forms will be absolutely worthless, whether on human action itself, or on the efforts put forth by the Church for directing it. When an uneducated rustic can form a just criticism on the poetical beauty of Hamlet or Faust, then (and not till then) will it be worth while to listen to our poor blinded intellectualist, when he expresses his judgment on the maxims and policy of the Holy See. Such men have already pronounced on the Church the very highest eulogium which it is in their power to pronounce, when they have expressed a severe censure on her rules and principles, and a kind of compassionate contempt for her divinely appointed pastors.

In our article on "Rome and the Munich Congress,"* we have assumed, as a matter of course, that the Ecclesia Docens is infallible, not merely when she condemns propositions as heretical, but also when she brands them with certain lighter censures, such as "erroneous," "temerarious," and the like. It has occurred to us, however, since the article was printed off, that, as this assumption is the turning point of our whole argument, it will be more satisfactory if we adduce authority for our statement. The following passage from De Lugo will be amply sufficient for our purpose :—

"Communiter . . . doctores fatentur certum esse Ecclesiæ judicium in his censuris statuendis. Banes . . . dicit esse errorem, vel errori proximum, dicere *posse Ecclesiam in eo judicio errare.* Malderus . . . dicit hæreticum esse qui id pertinaciter affirmaret. P. Coninck . . . dicit valdè probabilem esse hanc Malderi sententiam. P. Luisius Turianus . . . dicet esse *errorem* dicere quòd in his censuris decernendis *possit Pontifex Summus errare.* . . . Ego etiam id puto *vel esse erroneum vel errori proximum ;* quia *infallibilis Spiritûs Sancti assistentia* Ecclesiæ promissa non videtur limitanda ad ea solùm dogmata quæ tanquam de fide proponuntur et creduntur ab Ecclesiâ, sed debet extendi ad ea omnia quæ fideles *ex præcepto Ecclesiæ credere tenentur.*—*De Fide,* d. 20, n. 108, 9.

This statement is undeniable and unquestionable. According to Catholic doctrine, the Ecclesia Docens is infallible, not only (1) as "testis," *i.e.,* as witness of

---

* July, 1864. Note to the preceding article, p. 217.

Apostolic Dogma, but also (2) as "judex," *i.e.*, as judge of the controversies referring thereto; and (3) as "magistra," *i.e.*, as the authoritative guide to Christian truth and practice. Now it is most plain that she would not be infallible as "magistra," if she could authoritatively denounce propositions as theologically censurable which do not in fact deserve that censure.

ESSAY II.*

THE POPE'S DECLARATION ON HIS CIVIL PRINCEDOM.

THIS work† is an enlargement of some papers which appeared last year in the *Civiltà Cattolica.* It occupies a ground which is singularly important at the present time, not only in regard to the Pope's civil princedom, but to many other subjects also; and its reasoning has a close affinity with that which we have ourselves pursued in this number on the Munich Brief.

At the time when so much excitement existed among good Catholics on the Pope's civil princedom, there must have been some even well-educated men, who felt themselves unable to form any judgment of their own; and had no other wish in the matter, than simply to accept the declarations of ecclesiastical authority, in

* July, 1864. From "Notices of Books," pp. 218—220.

† "Il Valore e la Violazione della Dichiarazione Pontificia sopra il Dominio Temporale della S. Sede." Per il P. Valentino Steccanella, D.C.D.G. Roma.

the very way in which such authority desired their acceptance. But there was some little difficulty in understanding what that precise way was: in understanding, *e.g.*, how far such authority required from the faithful *their interior assent*, and (if so) to what exact doctrine. This difficulty, we venture to think, did not receive all the attention which it deserved; and F. Steccanella deserves our best thanks, for treating it so frankly and intelligibly.

The foundation of his argument is the Holy Father's authoritative statement, put forth in the Encyclical of June 18th, 1859. "We publicly declare (*palam edicimus*) that the civil princedom is necessary to this Holy See, in order that she may exercise her sacred power for the good of religion without any impediment." Two explanations, however, must be added, if we would rightly apprehend the Pope's meaning in this judgment. Firstly, he does not, of course, say that the civil princedom is necessary for the Church's *existence*, as though God had promised that it should never be taken away; but only that it is necessary for the unimpeded exercise of her sacred power, and so for her well-being (see Steccanella, p. 135). And, secondly, he does not mean that the civil princedom is necessary even for this end, under all imaginable circumstances; but under the particular circumstances of modern society. So he has expressly explained himself in the Apostolical Letter of March 26th, 1860. "Since," he says, "in order to act with due freedom, she needed those helps which suited *the condition and necessity of the times*, it came to pass by an admirable counsel of divine providence, that when the Roman empire fell and was divided into many kingdoms, the

Roman Pontiff obtained a civil princedom. By which circumstance it was most wisely provided by God himself, that, amidst so great a multitude and variety of temporal kings, the Supreme Pontiff should enjoy that political liberty, which is so greatly necessary for the unimpeded exercise of his spiritual power over the whole world."

The declaration of the Holy Father, which we began by citing, was undoubtedly put forth by him, not as a private doctor, but as Universal Teacher; and the whole Catholic Episcopate has expressly or tacitly given assent. Both these statements are absolutely evident, from the address presented by the great multitude of bishops assembled at Rome on June 8th, 1862. "But," they say, "it is scarcely becoming in us to speak more at length on this so grave matter; in us, who have often heard thee, not so much discussing it, as [authoritatively] teaching on the subject. For thy voice, as a sacerdotal trumpet, hath loudly proclaimed to all the world that 'the temporal power is providential;' *it must, therefore, be held by us all as most certain* that this rule hath accrued to the Holy See, not fortuitously, but by a special Providence, &c. &c." No one has affected to doubt, that the bishops then present at Rome did but represent, in so expressing themselves, the judgment of their absent brethren also. The bishops themselves, therefore, proclaim that, in consequence of the Pope's declaration, they are under the obligation of "holding most certainly" the doctrine which it enounces; in other words, they proclaim that it is a declaration which demands our firm interior assent. Since, on the Church's authority, therefore, the Ecclesia Docens requires our firm interior assent to this declaration, on the Church's authority, it follows, even on Gallican principles, that Catholics are bound to yield such assent. Catholics are not, indeed, required or permitted, as our author observes (p. 88), to invest this proposition with the certainty of divine faith; but they *are* required to regard it as indubitably certain in a lower grade. Its pertinacious disbelief would not involve the guilt of heresy, but it *would* deserve some lighter theological censure.

An objection, of course, is at once raised against this conclusion; viz., that the whole question is external to the limits of the Apostolic Depositum, and that the Ecclesia Docens therefore possesses no infallibility in its decision. The most valuable part of the present work consists of its various replies to this critical objection. We cannot, indeed, here attempt any detailed analysis of these replies; but we will give a general notion of their character. Our author maintains strenuously that the Ecclesia Docens is infallible, not only in those matters which directly concern dogma, but in those also which indirectly concern it. It is most certain that the Church may not only declare infallibly the Catholic doctrine on any head, but may also denounce infallibly some given book, as adverse to such doctrine in its drift and tendency. No one, indeed, but a heretic, can deny this. In like manner, argues our author, she may not only declare infallibly the extent of her own powers, but she may also declare infallibly that certain given external circumstances are inconsistent with the unimpeded exercise of those powers.* True, the Apostles never taught

* Since the recent Encyclical and Syllabus, it is more satisfactory

the Church that under certain future circumstances the civil princedom would be necessary; but neither did they teach the Church, that a certain book would be written by a certain Jansenius in the sixteenth century, which would contain five certain erroneous propositions.

The one conclusive answer, however, to the above-named objection is, of course, that on which F. Steccanella lays his principal stress. The Ecclesia Docens *does* regard the Pope's declaration as demanding our interior assent. If she were mistaken in her teaching on this head, she would be mistaken on a matter which is directly and exclusively doctrinal; viz., the limit of her own prerogative.

---

perhaps to express this somewhat differently. In the "Quantâ curâ," the Pope claims infallibility for those "judgments" which "regard the Church's rights, discipline, and general good." In page 7, we have supported the Church's general claim of infallibility in her minor censures, by urging that, without such gift she could not adequately preserve the purity of that Faith which is committed to her keeping. In like manner we may support the claim, put forth in the "Quantâ curâ," by arguing, that unless she possessed infallibility in those "judgments" pronounced by her which "regard the Church's rights, discipline, and general good," she could not adequately secure those rights, vindicate that discipline, and promote that general good.

ESSAY III.*

INFALLIBILITY CLAIMED FOR THE ENCYCLICAL "MIRARI VOS."

THE Encyclical "Mirari vos," as is well known, was issued by Gregory XVI. on occasion of his mounting the Pontifical throne; and comprises, among its other contents, an emphatic condemnation of certain errors advocated by Lamennais. It is no part of our present purpose to treat Lamennais's movement historically; we shall not inquire either into the grounds of his great influence, or into its permanent effects.† We shall here consider his acts and writings, so far only as they illustrate the claim on a Catholic's interior assent, possessed by certain doctrinal declarations in the Encyclical. In order, however, that our readers may understand the use which we desire to make of Lamennais's works, it will be necessary to make a few preliminary observations.

* January, 1865. From an article called "Extent of the Church's Infallibility—the Encyclical 'Mirari vos'," pp. 41-58, 68, 69.

† Some very interesting remarks on Lamennais will be found in the preface to Professor Robertson's recent work, "Lectures on Some Subjects of Modern History and Biography," pp. xii—xiv.

No one is a Catholic at all, who does not attribute infallibility to the collective body of Catholic bishops, when professing to teach the Catholic Faith, as such, in union with their head. But there are two propositions which may be held by a Catholic, at all events, without forfeiting his title to Catholicism. He may hold (1), that the Holy See is not infallible, even in those definitions of *faith* which it may put forth, unless the Catholic Episcopate expressly or tacitly adhere to them; and he may hold (2), that Pope and bishops united are fallible, when they condemn a thesis, not precisely as heretical, but as deserving some lesser censure. The former proposition constitutes what is commonly called the Gallican doctrine; nor have we any intention here of speaking against it. We do not, indeed, see how this doctrine can have any practical bearing on our controversies of the present time; when the great body of bishops are so loyal to the Holy Father, and so convinced of his infallibility, that they assent, as a matter of course, to his authoritative declarations.* But the second proposition, on the contrary, raises a question, which was never so momentous as now; since at this particular period the chief danger to dogma arises, as is constantly remarked, from philosophical rather than from theological error. In order, therefore, to concentrate our attention on this particular question, and to prevent our readers from

---

* Even on a point which no one alleges to be an integral part of the Depositum—the necessity, under actual circumstances, of the Pope's civil princedom—the bishops assembled in Rome (June 8th, 1862), say to the Holy Father, "Thy voice hath loudly proclaimed, &c., *it must therefore be held by us all as most certain.*"

mixing it up in any way with the old Gallican discussions, we will suppose throughout, that every Papal utterance, for which we claim infallibility, has been fully accepted and assented to, at least tacitly, by the body of Catholic bishops. It would tend to wearisome prolixity, if we expressly mentioned this in every instance; we would, therefore, request our readers to understand that such condition is invariably implied.

We will enter, then, at once on the question before us; and will begin with one or two obvious but necessary explanations. When a thesis is condemned as heretical, its contradictory is thereby asserted as an integral part of the Catholic Faith; and, conversely, every definition of faith implies a condemnation of the contradictory tenet as heretical. It is evident, however, that there may be many false theses, which are not in themselves heretical, but which lead by legitimate consequence to heresy; and many others which, though not leading to it by strictly legitimate consequence, are yet so connected with it in spirit and tendency that, unless expelled from Catholic thought, they will certainly introduce it. Now it is the duty of the Ecclesia Docens, not merely to preserve the Deposit pure at any given period, but to watch jealously against the entrance of any dangerous element, which may hereafter be injurious to such purity. Accordingly she brands such theses as the above, but with less severe censures; they are pronounced "erroneous," "temerareous," and the like, according to the particular kind and degree of their theological unsoundness.

Now, if she be infallible, as we are about to maintain, not only in her censure of heresy, but in these inferior censures also, it follows that there is an enormous number of *philosophical* truths, on which she may infallibly pronounce; and this because of their intimate connection with the Apostolical Deposit. We gave our reasons for this statement in our last July number (see pp. 13, 14 of this volume), and we need not therefore here repeat our argument. But further, there are certain *facts*, over and above those recorded in Scripture, on which, for the same reason, the Church may pronounce with equal authority. Of these "dogmatical facts" (as they are called), the most celebrated instance is found in the history of Jansenism. Five propositions were taken from Jansenius's "Augustinus," and condemned mostly as heretical. The Jansenists admitted the heterodoxy of these five propositions, but denied that any one of the number could be found in Jansenius's book; and they argued, that the Church had no authority to control their interior belief on this head, because it was a question, not of doctrine, but of fact. The answer was obvious. Jansenius's book was so saturated with heresy and error, that whoever accepted it as orthodox, would certainly imbibe the five condemned propositions, even though he should fancy himself not to hold them. This was quite imaignable and credible, apart from any decision of the Church; and it is now infallibly certain, because the Church decreed those to be implicated in the Jansenistic heresy who were wrong on the question of fact, no less than those who might be explicitly wrong on the question of doctrine. Here, indeed, was a case, in which those who refused assent to the Church's declaration of fact, were accounted actual heretics; it will therefore be more directly to our purpose, if we subjoin another instance, where this extreme censure is not in question. If the opinion should obtain a footing in the Church, that the Pope's civil princedom is not now necessary for the due performance of his spiritual functions, a most false impression would gain ground, as to the real extent and character of those functions: the question of fact is connected with the question of doctrine. This also was imaginable and credible apart from any decision of the Church; but (as we must maintain) is infallibly certain now that the Church has spoken.* Canonization again, is another instance in point.† From all this, then, it follows that, as there is a class of *directly* doctrinal truths, viz., those which are actual parts of the Apostolic Deposit; so also there is a class of truths *indirectly* doctrinal, viz., those which are intimately bound up and connected with the former. We would beg our readers, therefore, to bear in mind, that wherever in this article we use the word "doctrine" and its derivatives, we intend to include *both* the above-named classes.

There are various methods, by which the Holy

---

* See our notice of F. Steccanella's work last July (pp. 30—34 of this volume). See, however, note at p. 33.

† "Some things have no connection with the subject of faith and morals, referring to the whole Church; but there are other things which have such connection. And, therefore, though the Roman Pontiff may sometimes be deceived *in facts* of the former class, *the reverse is to be said as to facts of the second class*, among which canonization is counted."—Benedict XIV., *De Canonisatione Sanctorum*, lib. 1, c. 44, n. 4. Since this was first published, the whole question of dogmatical facts has been admirably and most comprehensively handled by Dr. Murray, of Maynooth, in his "Treatise on the Church."

Father is in the habit of uttering those lesser censures which are our special subject. Sometimes he does so, by expressly ordering some decree of a Roman congregation to be promulgated; sometimes by a declaration emanating directly from himself. Then as to his immediate decisions, we find that they are given in two different ways. In many cases he puts out a formal decree; he accurately specifies or "formulises" the objectionable tenets; and censures them with no less precision and solemnity, than he uses in condemning heresy itself. Thus (to mention no other instances), Alexander VIII., in his decrees of Sept. 24, 1665, and March 18, 1666, having recounted 45 theses, "condemns and prohibits them as being at least scandalous;" and Innocent XII. makes 23 extracts from Fénélon's work, pronouncing them respectively scandalous, erroneous, &c. Nay, it often happens, as in Leo X.'s condemnation of Luther, Clement XI.'s of Quesnel, and many others, that the very same document condemns certain theses as heretical, and others as unsound in some lesser degree. Here, then, we have one kind of Papal declaration, containing a formulised teaching and a formulised censure. But not all Papal censures are delivered in this form. Thus Pius IX.'s condemnation of Frohschammer, and, again, the Munich Brief, were in the form of a letter addressed to the Archbishop of Munich; his more specific condemnation of Günther was contained in a letter addressed to the Archbishop of Cologne; and neither of the three was expressed in that technical, and (as it were) legal, form, with which the former class of censures is invested. Thus also the "Mirari vos," with which we are more immediately concerned, is in form merely the customary Encyclical issued by Gregory XVI. on his accession; while it is written throughout in a free, flowing, and rhetorical style. A large number of similar instances might easily be added.

Now certain Catholics hold that even the Pope's formulised judgment, confirmed by that of the whole Catholic Episcopate, is fallible, so far as it pronounces any censure less severe than that of "heretical." So extreme an opinion, however, must always be confined to a very small number; and we need not argue against it, because all which we shall presently urge for the infallibility of less formal declarations, applies *à fortiori* to these more solemn and formulised censures. We will only pause briefly to show how strong is the authority of theologians in our favour. De Lugo, for instance, thus writes :—

> Doctors commonly confess that the Church's judgment is certain in pronouncing these [lesser] censures. Bañes says that it is *error, or close upon error*, to say that *the Church can err in that judgment.* Malderus says that *he would be a heretic who should pertinaciously affirm this.* Father Coninch says that *this opinion of Malderus is very probable.* Father Luisius Turrianus says that *it is error to say* that the Supreme Pontiff can err in these censures. I also think this either erroneous or close upon error; because *the infallible assistance of the Holy Ghost promised to the Church* is not, as it seems, to be limited to those dogmata alone which are proposed and believed by the Church as of faith, but should be extended to all those things which the faithful are bound to believe by the Church's precept."—*De Fide*, d. 20, n. 108 and 109.*

Viva's name must be added to the list of those who regard it as actually heretical to deny that a thesis infallibly merits that censure which the Church pro-

* See the original quoted by us last July (p. 28 of this volume).

nounces on it. Lastly, Benedict XIV., a theologian so singularly characterized by caution and moderation, is not less peremptory against that opinion which would confine the Church's infallibility to a mere interpretation of the Depositum. His subject, indeed, does not lead him to treat of censures in general: but he holds it as absolutely certain, that the Pope is infallible in the canonization of a saint; adding that the only doubt is, whether a denial of this infallibility be actually heretical, or only censurable in some lower degree.*

These foundations having been laid, we will state as definitely as we can the proposition for which we are about to contend. Let us suppose the Pope to put out some declaration which, whatever its form, is intended for publication (as is shown by the circumstances of the case), with the purpose of inculcating some doctrine on the whole Church as theologically certain, or of denouncing some tenet to the whole Church as theologically unsound. Let us also suppose that the Catholic Episcopate in general, expressly or tacitly, assents to this declaration. We maintain that the doctrine so inculcated is infallibly true, and that the tenet so denounced infallibly merits that particular censure which has been expressed; and that the contrary opinion is theologically unsound. We wish it, however, to be distinctly understood, that in this article (as already implied) we are concerned only with actual documents emanating from the Holy See: any

---

* Viva, *De Thesibus damnatis quæstio prodroma*, n. 18. Benedict XIV., *De Canonisatione Sanctorum*, lib. 1, c. 43—45. See specially the last paragraph, c. 45, n. 28.

other doctrinal decisions—such, for instance, as are involved in the Pope's promulgating some decree of a Pontifical Congregation—are external to our present argument.

For our proposition, then, as we have stated it, we will give three reasons, any one of which we are persuaded would by itself be amply sufficient.

Ask any theologians of repute what are those cases in which a doctrinal utterance of the Holy Father is not infallible. They will reply that it is not infallible, unless he put it forth in his capacity of Universal Teacher; and they will add, if they are Gallicans, that it is not infallible unless the general body of bishops assent. No other exceptions have been ever suggested; and no other can be supposed without manifest theological unsoundness. Yet the case which we are contemplating cannot be included under either without an absolute contradiction of terms.

Then, secondly, he who accepts Catholicism, by that very fact accepts the Ecclesia Docens as his infallible guide to heaven. Now the Ecclesia Docens (so we assume) teaches that certain doctrines are infallibly true, as being integral parts of the Catholic Faith; and that certain others are infallibly true, as being indissolubly bound up with the former. On what imaginable ground can any one accept her testimony to the former class, while he rejects her testimony to the latter? If she is mistaken in considering herself infallible on one class of questions, how can we take her word for her infallibility on another? No one, it is plain, could adopt such a notion, without the gravest theological error: it leads by most necessary and immediate consequence to actual heresy.

These two arguments are so very obvious and irresistible, that we believe no Catholic really rejects our proposition as it stands. It is true, indeed, as we have already observed, that some few deny the Church's infallibility in pronouncing, ever so solemnly, a censure short of "heretical;" and that many deny her infallibility in those less formal declarations, which we are particularly considering. But, when pressed, they will allege, we believe, that the Ecclesia Docens does not herself claim such infallibility.* Specially in regard to such pronouncements as the "Mirari vos," they will express themselves somewhat as follows:—"The Pope" (they will say) "on such occasions addresses the faithful, as a father, who claims no infallibility, might address his children. The Pope puts before Catholics his deep conviction on some doctrinal or practical matter; and his conviction undoubtedly deserves most respectful consideration, from the elevated position of him who expresses it. He exhorts them to ponder well its grounds, and forbids them, at all events, openly to contradict it; but more than this he neither requires nor wishes."

This is an allegation of fact, and can only be met by an appeal to fact. It is for this reason that we shall call Lamennais into court, that he may testify the purport of his own condemnation; and we will show, in the sequel of this article, by evidence absolutely

* Zallinger, in a passage repeatedly quoted, lays down the principle which we believe that at least very few Catholics will expressly deny:—"Papal constitutions have force only in that sense and within those limits to which the Pope intended them to be confined." Our acceptance of them should not go beyond the Pope's intentions; but neither (by parity of reason) should it fall short of those intentions.

irresistible, that Gregory XVI., in the "Mirari vos," professed nothing less than to pass an infallible judgment on the errors brought before him, in his capacity of S. Peter's successor. We believe that the same can be shown as to other Papal utterances of the same character, in almost every individual instance. But such a procedure is surely unnecessary; for there is no human being who will admit the doctrinal infallibility of this Encyclical, while he hesitates in attributing the same quality to that whole class of Papal decrees which it represents. In fact, there is no one objection brought against the authority of other decrees, which does not emphatically apply to this. The Papal judgment is not formally addressed to the Universal Church, but only to the bishops. It does not purport to be a dogmatic decree, but an Encyclical issued on occasion of Gregory's accession. Passing from its form to its actual contents, they consist in an enumeration of the principal evils which at that period afflicted the Church; and one half of it contains no allusion whatever, either to Lamennais in particular, or to disputed doctrine in general. When we come to that writer's condemnation, there is no attempt at precise and scientific analysis, whether of the tenets condemned, or of the contrary truths inculcated; but rather a copious flow of rhetoric—most impressive, indeed, and beautiful, but still rhetoric—and a certain tone of pious excitement, very different from that which pervades definitions of faith. Lastly, neither directly nor by implication are the condemned tenets branded as actually heretical. No other such Papal declaration of doctrine, then, with which we are acquainted, admits of so many plausible objections against its infallibility as does this, of which, as we shall see, Gregory XVI. directly affirmed, at a later period, that he had issued it as a final and infallible judgment.

Before entering, however, on the facts of this particular controversy, we must conclude our general course of theological remark. And here it may not be misplaced, if we subjoin one or two other instances, which may be sufficiently set forth without exceeding our allotted space, and which abundantly show how mistaken are those who think that the Popes do not claim infallibility for this class of decisions. Take, for instance, the following passage addressed by Pope Alexander VII. to the Rector of Louvain University:—

> Unless *all the thoughts and devices* (cogitationes et consilia) of men, and specially of men of study (literis addictorum), *adhere immovably* in the case of *all Apostolical determinations without exception* (in omnibus omnino determinationibus Apostolicis) to the firmness of that rock on which the Lord hath built the foundations of the Church, it is quite incredible into how many and great follies and insanities the activity (curiositas) of man's intellect is carried along a trackless way; and that the more, in proportion to the excellence of its strength and perspicacity.*

So Pius IX., when repeating his condemnation of Günther, says:—

> The original censure of that philosopher's works by the Congregation of the Index, sanctioned as it was by our authority and *published by our command*, ought to have been amply sufficient, in order that the whole question should be regarded as having received its final decision (penitùs dirempta censeretur), and that all who glory in the Catholic name should clearly and distinctly understand, that obedience was altogether due, and that the doctrine contained in Günther's books *might not be esteemed sound* (sinceram haberi non posse).

And at a later period, as we observed in our July

* Quoted by Cardinal Pacca to Lamennais, vol. xii. p. 129.

number (p. 10 of this volume), he states as a *reductio ad absurdum* of some proposition which he censures, that to uphold it would be to imply that his condemnation of Günther had been erroneous.* Then again, so lately as December 19, 1861, in addressing the Archbishop of Malines on some philosophical controversies connected with traditionalism, which had caused much excitement, he uses these words:—

Wherefore, expressing no opinion whatever on the merit of those doctrines which have excited the present controversy, and *of which the definitive examination and judgment belong absolutely* (*unicè*) *to this Apostolic See*, we will and command that, *until this Holy See shall have thought fit to express a definitive judgment on this teaching*, both their favourers and their impugners shall abstain from professing and defending any one of those *philosophical* and theological doctrines, as that which is *the one doctrine*, *the true doctrine*, the doctrine alone to be admitted and characteristic of the Catholic University (veluti unicam veram, et solam admittendam, ac veluti Catholicæ universitatis propriam).

Here he undeniably implies, that whenever the Holy See should "express a definitive judgment on this teaching," the doctrine so determined will *rightly* be upholden, as that which is the one doctrine, the true doctrine, *the doctrine alone to be admitted.*

But there is a more general consideration, which is decisive; viz., the notorious circumstance that such Pontifical declarations are never afterwards modified or revoked, though they may, no doubt, be authoritatively explained. Those pronouncements on doctrine which are but disciplinary may, of course, be reversed.

* Our readers should be reminded that the declaration for which the Pope thus claims inerrancy, was in form precisely similar to the late Munich Brief. It was addressed to an individual pastor, the Archbishop of Cologne.

Thus John XXII., not only as a private doctor inclined to the opinion that the Beatific Vision is not enjoyed before the resurrection of the body, but as Pope forbade any one to be molested for that opinion, under the then circumstances ;* his successor defined the contradictory doctrine as of faith. All discussion on those controversies which relate to the "auxilia" of Grace, was once forbidden, except by special permission ; but there is no longer any such prohibition. But, on the other hand, who ever dreams of its being possible that at some future time a Catholic will be allowed to advocate the system of Günther, or of Frohschammer, or that condemned in the Munich Brief? Yet how is it possible to explain this contrast, except by the obvious solution, that the latter class are regarded by the Pope, not as disciplinary enactments, but as final and infallible determinations of Catholic truth ?

And this brings us to the third argument in support of our original proposition; viz., its effect on the reception of philosophical truth. Even in our own memory, how many philosophical propositions have been condemned by the Holy See !—Hermes's general system and various individual propositions; Lamennais's general system ;† Günther's general system and various individual propositions ; French traditionalistic error; and others. Now we, who regard all these condemnations as infallibly just, hail them with joy;

* Raynaldus, A.D. 1333, n. 467, "donec aliud ordinatum per Sedem Apostolicam fuerit vel declaratum ;" *i.e.*, "until the Holy See should issue either a different *command*, or else a doctrinal *declaration*."

† We are not referring here to the "Mirari vos," but to a later Encyclical, dated July 10, 1834.

because every accession to the Church's stock of infallible truth is a matter of congratulation. But what have our opponents to say on the subject? They admit the duty of respectful silence towards any such declaration, but deny its infallibilty. We may remind them of the obvious fact, that truth is one but error multiform; and consequently that every true philosophical proposition is the one exclusive truth, on that special question which it immediately treats. Their theory, therefore, amounts to this:—The Holy Father enjoys no infallible guidance in his judgment on these philosophies; but he is at liberty to select an indefinite and ever-increasing number of philosophical propositions, and to condemn them. From the moment of their condemnation to the end of the world, no Catholic will be allowed publicly to defend them, or even profess his belief in them; and in all Catholic colleges every philosophical student will be taught that they are philosophically false and theologically dangerous: while, nevertheless, there is every probability (since the Pope has no infallible guidance in selecting them) that several of their number express the one exclusive truth, on those questions which they immediately treat. Strange, indeed, is such a theory; but still stranger that it should be upholden by thinkers, who profess to advocate with peculiar earnestness the unspeakable preciousness of truth and of intellectual liberty. In the name of truth they uphold a theory which hopelessly mixes up truth with falsehood; and in the name of liberty they advocate an intellectual despotism, than which none ever was imagined, speculatively more unreasonable, or practically more grinding and intolerable.

It is quite impossible that men can remain for ever fixed in so false a position. The ground—who can tell how soon?—must be felt by them as slipping from under their feet; they must take a step backward, or a step in advance. We live in anxious times.

But in order that our own views may be recommended to such men as these, nothing is more important than to avoid the least tinge of exaggeration. We will, therefore, add a few explanations, to make clearer what is the precise proposition for which we contend. We suppose all through that the Pope is intending to teach the whole Church some doctrine as theologically certain. In the case, therefore, of any given document, we have to consider, from the context and circumstances, which portion of it *expresses* such doctrine; for many statements, even doctrinal statements, may be introduced, not as authoritative determinations, but in the way of argument and illustration. (2.) Many Papal pronouncements, though they may introduce doctrinal reasons, yet are not doctrinal pronouncements at all, but disciplinary enactments; the Pope's immediate end in issuing them is, not that certain things may be believed, but that certain things may be done. If the doctrinal reasons even for a doctrinal declaration are not infallible, much less can infallibility be claimed for the doctrinal reasons of a disciplinary enactment. (3.) Then, again, the Pope may give some doctrinal decision as Head of the Church, and yet not as Universal Teacher. Some individual may ask at his hands, and receive, practical direction on the doctrine to be followed in a particular case, while yet the Pope has no thought whatever of determining the question for the whole Church and for all time. (4.) Much less, as Benedict XIV. incidentally remarks,* does the fact of his acting officially on some moral opinion fix on it the seal of infallibility as certainly true. (5.) Nor, lastly, can any conclusive inference be drawn in favour of some doctrine or practice, from the fact of its not having been censured or prohibited. The Pontiff of the day, whether from intellectual or moral defect, may even omit censures and prohibitions which are greatly desirable in the Church's interest, or enact laws of an unwise and prejudicial character.

Yet, on the other hand, these qualifications must not be carried too far. As regards the last, for instance, it must never be forgotten, that the Holy Ghost most specially watches over S. Peter's See, and restrains within certain limits those evils which might follow from the mistakes and shortcomings of its occupant. Then, again, although a single doctrinal answer, given *e. g.* to an individual bishop and not published by the Pope, is not infallible,—a series of similar answers, given by different Popes under great variety of time and circumstance, may well be so considered; and there can be no doubt that the unchanged and fundamental maxims of Papal government are infallibly sound. Moreover, the Pope is infallible, not only in teaching faith and morals, but in universal discipline; or, in other words, he is not permitted to make a law for the Church, which cannot be obeyed consistently with sound doctrine and true moral principle.

We are not here going to argue in support of the statements contained in the last two paragraphs; we

* *De Canonisatione*, l. 1, c. 42, n. 13.

have but made those statements, as fixing more precisely the limits and bearing of that proposition, which our argument is directed to maintain. Nor even yet is our necessary explanation complete, till we have said a word on such doctrinal decrees as are put forth by the Pontifical Congregations. In an early number we hope to discuss at length this question, in connection with the critical case of Galileo. Here we will briefly state the conclusions which we are to advocate. Such decrees are not in themselves infallible: yet they possess the highest possible authority short of infallibility; insomuch that a loyal and well-disposed Catholic will yield to them, as a matter of course, a certain kind and degree of interior assent. Moreover, it not unfrequently happens that the Pontiff makes these decrees his own, by specially ordering their publication; as we have seen (p. 46 of this volume) on the first condemnation of Günther. In this case, we are disposed to consider that they become absolutely infallible.

Meanwhile an objection has been urged against our whole view, which some thinkers regard as very serious. They consider that "the gulf is infinite which separates what is of faith from what is not of faith;" and they allege very truly that our theory presents Catholic doctrine in a most different aspect. To us, their objection appears as unphilosophical as it is untheological. Is it the case in secular science, that a line can be broadly and sharply drawn, such that all on one side of that line is absolutely certain truth, while all on the other side is quite open and undetermined? Is not the opposite fact notorious? Some conclusions are absolutely established; others nearly so; others, again, under present circumstances, are much more probable than their contradictories, yet by no means sure not to be afterwards disproved; and so, along a kind of graduated scale, we finally arrive at those, on which as yet one side is not more probable than the other. So in theology. One class of doctrines unquestionably demands the assent of divine faith. Of a second class, it is quite certain that they are infallibly true, and probable that they are an actual part of the deposit. A third class are beyond all doubt infallibly true, yet with no pretensions to be strictly of faith. Of a fourth class, it is more or less probable that they are infallibly true. A fifth class are almost certainly true, though not infallibly determined. And so by degrees we arrive at those, on which every well-instructed Catholic has full liberty to take one side or the other. Thus the pursuit of theological science becomes one sustained discipline of intellectual docility; thus the student is constantly reminded, that he thinks under the assiduous superintendence and direction of that Holy See, whose continuous infallibility is the abiding light of Catholic doctrine.

We have argued, then, that not only certain doctrines are of faith,—but that certain others are infallibly determined by the Church to be true, as being intimately bound up with the former; and as the former class cannot be doubted without (at least material) mortal sin, so neither can the latter. It is always admitted, however, that where there is invincible ignorance of that authority on which the former class rest, the sin of non-belief is material only and not formal; and the same is even more obviously true as to the latter class. Here, moreover, an important distinction is to be noted. Those who are external to the Visible Church, however absolutely invincible their ignorance, cannot, of course, be admitted to Confession and Communion. But disbelief in those infallible decrees which are not definitions of faith, does not exclude from the body of the Church; and he, therefore, who is invincibly ignorant of the obligation to believe them, has full liberty of approaching the sacraments.

We are now to show, from the data furnished by Lamennais himself, that so far as regards him, the "Mirari vos" was not intended by Gregory XVI. as a mere disciplinary enactment commanding his silence; nor yet as a strong utterance of personal conviction; but as an infallible condemnation ex cathedrâ of that writer's erroneous system. All our extracts under this head will be from the twelfth volume, containing the "Affaires de Rome;" and we will begin with the time when he and his two friends (Lacordaire and Montalembert) were in that city, soliciting a judgment on the principles advocated in the *Avenir*. Under these circumstances, they addressed a memorial to the Holy Father, dated February 3, 1832; and no words can be plainer than those which follow, as showing that the judgment sought by them was to be no mere external regulation of their acts, but their rule of interior belief:—

O, father (they say), vouchsafe to cast your eye on some of the lowest of your children, who are accused of being rebellious against your *infallible* and mild authority. Behold them before you; read in their soul; there is nothing there for them to wish to hide. *If one of their thoughts, only one, differs from yours* (s'éloigne des vôtres), *they disavow, they abjure it.* You are the rule of their doctrines; never, no never, have they known others. O, father, pronounce over them that word which gives life *because it gives light*"— (p. 83).*

Lamennais waited till July, in hope of a decision; but he then left Rome, announcing that on his return he should continue the *Avenir*. He had not, however, gone farther than Munich, when he received a letter from Cardinal Pacca, dated August 16, inclosing a copy of the "Mirari vos," and informing him that his tenets were condemned therein (pp. 128-133). It is important to observe, that for all practical purposes this letter is to be considered as emanating from the Pope himself; for Cardinal Pacca calls it "the communication which his Holiness commissions me to forward to you in a confidential shape."† The cardinal says that his Holiness could the less decline to pronounce on the question, because "on every side the episcopate addressed itself to this Apostlic Chair to obtain *a solemn decision from the infallible mouth of S. Peter's successor* on certain doctrines of the *Avenir*." He refers Lamennais to the Encyclical itself, as specifying "the doctrines which his Holiness condemns *as contrary to the teaching of the Church;*" and, on the other hand, "*those which it is necessary to follow,*

* This passage had already appeared in the *Avenir* of Nov. 15, 1831; but they quote it in their memorial, as showing their true sentiments.

† It would appear that, according to usage, the Pope does not write personally to an ordinary Catholic, while under a cloud. All the communications from Gregory XVI. to Lamennais are addressed through some intermediary, until the latter made (as we shall see) his pretended submission; then comes a letter of congratulation, directly from the Pope.

according to holy and divine Tradition, and the constant maxims of the Apostolic See."

He ends a most touching letter with this beautiful passage:—

His Holiness remembers with very lively satisfaction the noble and solemn promise made by you, at the head of your *collaborateurs*, that you would imitate, according to our Saviour's precept, the humble docility of little children by *an unreserved submission* to the Vicar of Jesus Christ. That remembrance consoles his heart. I am sure that your promise will not fail. Thus you will console the afflicted heart of our Holy Father, restore peace and tranquillity to the clergy of France, ... and labour as God would have you (selon Dieu) for your solid celebrity, by imitating the example of that great man and prelate [Fénélon], the model of your nation, whose name will ever be dear and precious to the Church, and who was far more illustrious after his glorious act than before it. You will imitate, doubtless, that noble example: you are worthy of doing so. I felicitate you on this by anticipation, and seize with pleasure this opportunity of testifying to you my consideration, and showing you how much I am your very affectionate servant.

Here we interpose a comment. Lamennais, we have seen, appealed to the Pope's *infallible* authority; and the bishops desired "a solemn decision from the *infallible* mouth of S. Peter's successor." The Pope, says Cardinal Pacca, has acceded to this double request. To what request? There had been no request at all on either side, except that Gregory XVI. would pronounce an *infallible* judgment.

Lamennais at once gave up the *Avenir*, and dissolved an association which he had founded "for the defence of religious liberty;" on doing which, he received from the Pope a message of approval through F. Orioli, and another through Cardinal Pacca. But the cloven foot had already begun to show itself; for, in his address (p. 134) announcing his discontinuance of the *Avenir*, he very ominously refers to the Pope only as *Governor* of the Church, and avoids all allusion to him as her *Teacher*. "Hardly had my declaration appeared," he tells us (p. 137), "when men muttered words of distrust and discontent; it was not complete or explicit enough; it too much resembled the 'respectful silence' of the Jansenists:" or, in other words, the Catholic world began to suspect, that he rendered *obedience*, indeed, to the Pope's *command*, but not interior *assent* to his *teaching*. These suspicions soon reached Rome; and the Pope addressed thereon a letter to the Archbishop of Toulouse, dated May 8, 1833, which is so momentous, that we shall lay a considerable extract before our readers:—

> We read with much pleasure the letter which you sent to us on the 22nd of April last year [*i.e.*, before the "Mirari vos" was issued], in conjunction with other venerable brethren of the same nation. . . It was delivered to us at a time when we had ourselves long applied ourselves to that care and thought [which was necessary] that, according to the custom and practice of this Holy See, having gone through that . . . weighty examination which was needed by the very nature of the case, we might *opportunely teach all the children of the Church* what was to be preached, *according to the rule of sacred Scripture and holy Tradition*, on that most sad subject to which yours referred. For, remembering . . . . that our unworthiness presides over the Church, under his [S. Peter's] name *whose faith resists all errors*, we well understood, &c. . . . . This we faithfully performed by God's good help, and specially under the auspices of the most Holy Virgin, in the Encyclical Letter addressed on the solemn day of her Assumption to the Bishops of the Catholic world; in which, according to the duty of our office, we delivered that doctrine which is sound and *which alone it is lawful to follow* (sanam et quam unicè sequi fas sit doctrinam protulimus)—(pp. 359, 360).

Here, then, the Pope expressly states, that he had passed his judgment on Lamennais's errors *in his capacity of successor to S. Peter's infallibility;* that this judgment was intended *to teach all the children of the Church;* and that the doctrine thus delivered, derived as it is from Scripture and Tradition, is that *which alone it is lawful to follow.* Quid plura?

Gregory XVI. proceeds to express his grief at the reports in circulation, concerning those who were condemned in the Encyclical; and prays that God will give them a docile heart.

On receiving this letter from the Archbishop, Lamennais wrote to the Pope, begging for an explanation (pp. 138-140). He states to the Holy Father that his obedience has been complete; that the *Avenir* has ceased; that the objectionable society has been dissolved; that the subscribers have had back their money; that it is for the Chief of the Church alone to judge what is good and useful for her; and that he has resolved henceforward, in all his writings and acts, to remain totally external to ecclesiastical affairs. He concludes by craving instruction as to what he can say, in order fully to satisfy the Holy Father's requirements. The latter replied by a letter addressed to the Bishop of Rennes, and dated October 5, from which we will make a few extracts:—

> We are astonished that he has said these things. We were justly and deservedly distressed on finding the expectation deceived which that first act [of obedience] had raised; for we regarded that act as a herald by anticipation (prænuncium) of declarations [emanating from him], whereby it might be made manifest to the Catholic world that he *firmly and solidly holds* and professes (firmè et graviter tenere ac profiteri) that sound doctrine which we proposed in our Encyclical Letter—(p. 368).
>
> But this also was very grievous to us, that, whereas the same Lamennais acknowledged that it was our office to pronounce concern-

ing those things which are expedient to Catholic interests, he stated in his letter to us that he should henceforth be external, wherever there is a question concerning the Church and the cause of religion. For whither does this tend, venerable brother, except to this—that he reverences our supreme *authority*; but as yet does not show that he has submitted (obsecutum fuisse) to our *judgment* on this matter, and to *the doctrines declared by us*?

But we confess with joy that the promise now cheers us . . which Lamennais makes in the same letter, that he is prepared willingly and holily to profess those things, whereby we may be most certainly convinced of his *filial obedience.* He craves, therefore, to be instructed in words, whereby he may fully declare this his resolve. To which request we send one only reply; viz., that in regard to the doctrine delivered in our Encyclical Letter—wherein certainly . . . new precepts are not imposed, but only those things which have been established by Apostolic and Patristic Tradition—he should affirm (confirmet) that he *singly and absolutely follows it* (unicè et absolutè sequi), and will neither write *nor approve* anything at variance with it (nihil ab eâ alienum se aut scripturum esse aut probaturum)—pp. 370, 372.

On this Lamennais had recourse to a new device. He addressed a letter to the Pope (pp. 143, 144), professing the fullest deference to the teaching of the Holy See in spirituals, but adding that his conscience forbade him to yield such deference in temporals; and implying, that certain parts of the "Mirari vos" turned on matters purely temporal. This short letter he afterwards expanded into a memorial (pp. 147-153) which he forwarded to Rome through the Archbishop of Paris; and an answer was promptly received to it from Cardinal Pacca, acting again as the Pope's mouthpiece. The Pope had been persuaded, he says,—

that you would have followed the example of so many illustrious and learned men, of whom history has preserved to us the glorious remembrance; who, when they were accused of advancing aught false or inexact, immediately had recourse to the Apostolic See, and submitted themselves (s'en rapportaient) to the responses of *Peter's infallible mouth*: who, in the sacred person of his successors, imparts, and always will impart, *knowledge of the truth* to those who seek it in the spirit of humility and in sincerity.

The letter to the Bishop of Rennes informed you what declaration the common Father of the faithful expected from you, in order fully to satisfy him . . . . of your *unreserved and unequivocal adhesion* (adhésion illimitée et non équivoque) *to the doctrine of the Encyclical*—(p. 155).

The Pope had required of Lamennais, that he should promise to "follow" this doctrine "singly and absolutely;" and the cardinal adds, in the Pope's name, that he should yield to it an "unreserved and unequivocal adhesion." Things were thus brought to a crisis; and at this juncture occurs the strangest part of the whole history. In the work before us, Lamennais argues at length (pp. 157-165), against those parts of the Encyclical which condemn him; and declares that at that period "the more frequently he read it, the more he found his perplexities increase" (p. 159). In this state of mind, he went to the Archbishop of Paris; and (as he tells us, for the sake of peace) subscribed the following declaration:—

I, the undersigned, in that very form of words which is contained in the Brief of the Supreme Pontiff, Gregory XVI., dated Oct. 5, 1833, affirm that I singly and absolutely follow the doctrine declared in the same Pontiff's Encyclical Letter, and that I will neither write nor approve anything at variance with it—(p. 166, note).

The Pope, on hearing of this, sent him at once a letter of overflowing joy and affectionateness, which, one would think, must have bowed him to the earth with shame. This letter was dated Dec. 28, 1833. Lamennais showed his sincerity and gratitude, by occupying the earlier part of the very next year in writing his abominable "Paroles d'un Croyant"; against which the Pope directed an indignant Encyclical, dated July 10, 1834 (pp. 381-410). It is important for our purpose to point out, that in this latter Encyclical the Pope uses the strong word "*defined*" (definivimus) (p. 390), in speaking of that "*Catholic doctrine*" which he had delivered in the "Mirari vos."

We would further add that, as Lamennais expressly states, and as indeed is notorious, the whole doctrine of the Encyclical was "adopted by the bishops, not one of whom uttered a single word of protest" (p. 294). And we will appeal, in conclusion, to any one of our readers, whatever may be his shade of theological opinion, whether the facts which we have adduced do not abundantly and superabundantly establish the conclusion, for which we have adduced them.

* * * * * * * *

Our object in now drawing attention to the "Mirari vos" has been to vindicate the infallibility appertaining to its doctrinal declarations; and this not principally for their own sake, but rather for the sake of that whole class of ecclesiastical utterances which they represent and exemplify. This vindication we hope we have satisfactorily accomplished; and it only remains here to notice an objection which has reached us, from more than one quarter, in regard to similar statements put forth in our article of last July, on "Rome and the Munich Congress." It has been objected, that no important end is gained, while divisions are generated and increased, by obtruding on notice a doubtful and extreme theory. We must profess ourselves quite unable to understand the grounds of this objection. Consider the vast number of politico-religious questions, such as those determined in the "Mirari vos;" consider, again, the vast number of philosophical questions, such as those involved in the condemnation of Hermes and of Günther: how enormous is their reach, and how profound their influence! The whole mental attitude of an educated Catholic, towards the Church and towards Rome, is absolutely revolutionized, when he comes round from the contrary opinion to that of regarding her as infallible on such questions. At this moment a great interest is felt, as to providing a higher education for our gentry; and much difference of opinion prevails, on the best method of doing so. But on one point all thinkers must be unanimous; viz., in counting it among the most momentous necessities of our time, that such education should inculcate true doctrine on the extent of the Church's infallibility, whatever they may consider such true doctrine to be. Never was there a controversy which it is less possible to ignore. Certainly, to insist on a doubtful theory as though it were certain, is most unjustifiable, and tends to schism; but to treat a closed question as though it were an open one, is no less unjustifiable, and tends to heresy.

Those who refuse unreserved interior submission to these ecclesiastical declarations,—and those who fall into the kindred error of denying their due theological authority to the Pontifical Congregations,—are usually, so far as we have observed, insensible to any amount of direct argument, from their concentration of thought on one particular fact of the past, viz., Galileo's condemnation. They regard this fact as decisive: it deprives us, they think, of so much as a standing ground in controversy, and justifies them in pooh-poohing us out of court. In a very early number, therefore, we will carefully consider that condemnation, so far as it has any bearing on these truly momentous questions.

ESSAY IV.*

INFALLIBILITY CLAIMED FOR THE RECENT ENCYCLICAL AND SYLLABUS.

HARDLY any Pontificate, in the whole history of the Church, has so abounded in important doctrinal pronouncements, as that of Pius IX. Firstly, he has put forth an actual definition of faith; and that, too, distinguished from all others, by more than one characteristic circumstance. Alone among such definitions (as has been often observed) it condemned no existing error; insomuch that the Catholic's joy and exultation, at this fresh proclamation of divinely revealed Truth, was saddened by no regret for condemned heretics, or for brethren fallen from the faith. Then, again, never was there a definition which exhibited in so clear a light the Church's august prerogative, of developing implicit dogma into an explicit portion of the One Faith. For how was the doctrine of Our Lady's Immaculate Conception circumstanced, during that eventful December of 1854? On the 7th of that month no Catholic was *permitted* to stigmatize

* April, 1865. From an Article called "The Enyclical and Syllabus," pp. 441—450, 498, 499.

its denial as *unsound;* on the 8th, all Catholics were *required* to regard such denial as *heretical.*

With how much delight and gratitude Pius IX. contemplates the fact of his having been permitted to define that magnificent verity, is shown in the very Encyclical before us; for he dates it expressly and formally on the tenth anniversary of the definition. Yet his reign has been no less remarkable for those other doctrinal determinations, which, though not definitions of faith, yet peremptorily claim the unreserved interior assent of his spiritual children. The Church's whole doctrine on his civil princedom, as regards its methodical expression, has been commenced, matured, and perfected by him. And over how large a field of thought his other determinations have ranged, is emphatically testified by the document which he has now published. For the annexed Syllabus contains exclusively former pronouncements of Pius IX. himself; and every one, friend or foe, has been alike struck with the extent of ground which it covers.

And there is one circumstance which makes this fertility of authoritative doctrine peculiarly impressive and significant. It might have been expected, indeed, that the period of such fertility should have been one of much *intellectual* excitement and commotion; but no one could have anticipated so large an accession to theological first principles, unless the Pontiff were enjoying material peace and tranquillity. On the contrary, no Pontiff of modern times has been involved, through his whole reign, in so unrelenting a succession of political distresses. He has been "in peril from his own kindred, in peril from the nations, in peril from false brethren;" while burdened in a fuller sense than was S. Paul himself, with the "solicitude of all the Churches." Yet none of these things has lessened his zeal for doctrine. It was when an exile at Gaeta, that he first addressed himself to that definition of faith, which was to be the glory of his pontificate. And now, when the Franco-Italian Convention has been concluded, and his civil princedom is once more exposed to urgent and imminent peril, instead of seeking safety by silence and compromise, he expresses solemnly and stringently that very aspect of Christian truth, which will be most offensive to modern princes in general, and to the French Emperor in particular.

It is time, however, to pass from these general remarks, to that particular pronouncement which has given us the occasion of making them. The article of our last Number on the "Mirari vos" was written at a time when we had no expectation whatever of this new utterance from Rome; and yet had we known that such utterance was coming, we could hardly have better prepared the way for its due appreciation. In that article we treated on the noblest Encyclical ever issued by Gregory XVI.; and we have now to consider that which, if we include the Syllabus, will undoubtedly prove the noblest ever issued by his successor, even though the life of Pius IX. were prolonged for as many years, as his most affectionate children could desire. Not only (which is a matter of course) there is a deep identity of doctrine between the two; but there is no small resemblance, both in some of their attendant circumstances, and in the tone of indignant reprobation which they both display. In 1832, as in 1864, there were Catholics, filled with a zeal which is not according to knowledge, who maintained that the organization of modern society, with its characteristic "liberties," is the fullest exemplification of true social principle which the world has seen. In 1832, as in 1864, the reigning Pontiff did not content himself with condemning this monstrous exaggeration; but authoritatively decreed, that the speculative basis, on which those liberties are more commonly defended, is directly contrary to Catholic truth. If Gregory XVI. denounced as an "insanity" the tenet "that liberty of conscience is to be vindicated for each man," Pius IX. no less emphatically declares (prop. lxxix.) that the liberty of worships and of the press conduces to the corruption of morals and the propagation of a pestilential indifferentism. At the same time there is this very important difference between the two. Gregory XVI. put forth his Encyclical at the beginning of his reign; and its doctrinal decisions refer only to that particular error which was then in the ascendant. But Pius IX. is addressing the Church after many years of teaching and governing—years which have brought him into conflict with a vast and heterogeneous mass of hideous error. He now judges that the time has come for summing up the results of that conflict. He includes, therefore, in one large Apostolic denunciation, a great number of tenets, both philosophical and strictly theological; and he condemns them in company with those politico-religious errors, which altogether savour of the same school, though in themselves they are of course indefinitely less grievous, than the great majority of tenets herein censured.

And now as to the authority possessed by this Encyclical over the interior convictions of a Catholic. We have no hesitation in maintaining, consistently with our article on the "Mirari vos," that its doctrinal declarations possess absolute infallibility, in virtue of the promises made by Christ to S. Peter's Chair. Indeed, to hold that the Church's infallibility is confined to her definitions of faith, seems to us among the most fatal errors of the day; nor do we see where its legitimate results can stop, short of that extreme form of Catholic misbelief, which animated the late *Home and Foreign Review.* The tenet which would thus limit the Church's infallibility, is regarded by Viva and some other writers as heretical; several, such as Lugo, do not go so far as this, yet denounce it as theologically unsound; and theologians commonly (on Lugo's testimony) at all events reject it as untrue.* But a still stronger refutation of this tenet is supplied by the acts and words of the Holy See itself, than could be obtained by the united voice of all theologians. For instance, what words can be stronger and more explicit than those in which Gregory claimed infallibility for the "Mirari vos," of which no one ever dreamt that it was a definition of faith? Lamennais appealed in the first instance to the Pope's "*infallible*" authority;† and the Pope (through Cardinal Pacca) informed him that, in like manner, "on every side the episcopate" had "addressed itself to the Apostolic Chair to obtain a solemn decision from the *infallible* mouth of S. Peter's successor." The Pope acceded, he says, to this double request. To what request? There had been no request at all, except that Gregory would pronounce an *infallible* judgment on the doctrines in question.

* See p. 28 of this volume.

† Page 56 of this volume.

And in the following year he announced to the Archbishop of Toulouse that he had given the said decision as "presiding over the Church in his (S. Peter's) name, *whose faith resists all errors*,* *i. e.* as successor to S. Peter's *infallibility*. Afterwards, again through Cardinal Pacca, he complained that Lamennais had not "followed the example of so many" great men who "submitted themselves to the responses of *Peter's infallible mouth*."† The "Mirari vos," then, was regarded by him who issued it as a "response of Peter's infallible mouth." But if the "Mirari vos' is an infallible utterance of Peter, even more manifestly must this "Quantâ curâ," with its appended Syllabus, be so considered. As to the errors recited in the latter, their condemnation is as accurately "formulized"‡ as is Innocent XII.'s condemnation of Fénelon, or Alexander VIII.'s of relaxed morality. But even as to the Encyclical itself, there is throughout a far more manifest appearance on the surface than in the "Mirari vos" of its being intended as a doctrinal decree.§ Moreover, there occurs in it one very explicit statement, to which no parallel can be found in the earlier Encyclical,—a statement which can leave no possible doubt in any one's mind that the Holy Father is speaking ex cathedrâ as the Teacher of all Christians. "Therefore," he says, "by our Apostolic authority we reprobate, proscribe, and condemn all and singular the evil opinions and doctrines severally mentioned in this letter, and *will and command* that they be thoroughly (*omnino*) regarded *by all children of the Catholic Church* as reprobated, proscribed, and condemned." Such is

---

* p. 57. † p. 60. ‡ See p. 40 of this volume. § p. 45.

the relation between these two Encyclicals. Since, therefore, it is absolutely indubitable on Catholic principles that the doctrinal declarations issued by Gregory XVI. in the earlier one were infallibly true, there is no room for doubt or question that those now issued by Pius IX. are infallible also.*

But as on the one hand the "Quantâ curâ" falls in such sense under our argument of January, that its infallibility is thereby most firmly established;—so reciprocally the "Quantâ curâ" itself furnishes us with many signal confirmations of that argument. It gives us several further reasons (though surely no further reasons were needed) for holding, both that there is a class of infallible declarations altogether distinct from definitions of faith, and also that the said class is very far indeed from being either small in extent or inconsiderable in importance. Firstly, then, let the following extract be most carefully pondered:—

Nor can we pass over in silence the audacity of those who, not enduring sound doctrine, contend that without sin and without any sacrifice of the Catholic profession, assent and obedience may be refused to those judgments and decrees of the Holy See, whose object is declared to concern the Church's general good, and her rights and discipline, so only it do not touch the dogmata of faith and morals. But no one can be found not clearly and distinctly to see and understand, how grievously this is opposed to the Catholic dogma, of the full power given from God by Christ Himself to the Roman Pontiff, of feeding, ruling, and guiding the Universal Church.

---

* We so worded our former article all through, as to save the Gallican theory; for the purpose of making clearer the precise point which we maintained: but we never concealed our dissent from that theory. We admit, of course, that Gallicans cannot consistently regard the "Quantâ curâ" as infallible, until it has received express or tacit adhesion from the Episcopate.

Now those unsound Catholics who are at this time so dangerous, admit in theory that *obedience* is due to Papal *commands* of this character; but they are unanimous in maintaining that no *interior assent* is required, except to definitions of faith. It is most important, therefore, to point out, that reference is made in this passage to two different kinds of pronouncement from Rome; "judgments" which determine concerning truth or falsehood, and "decrees" or practical commands. For the former the Pope claims "assent" of the intellect; for the latter, "obedience" of the will. No one, we think, can read the sentence with candour, without seeing that such is its sense; but there is a further circumstance which establishes that sense beyond the possibility of doubt. Pius IX. declares that the error in question denies the Pope's true power of "*feeding* (*pascendi*), ruling, and guiding the Church." Now, what is the chief ecclesiastical sense of this word "pascendi"? It means principally "teaching;" and it is here fixed to that sense, by the circumstance that the Pope's other powers of "ruling and guiding" are separately mentioned.* Sound doctrine is constantly described under the figure of healthy pasture: the office of feeding, accordingly, is that of guiding the flock into healthy pasture, and preserving it from poisonous herbage; or, in other words, and dropping the metaphor, of inculcating truth and denouncing error. The image in question may be found fully drawn out in the opening sentence

* A passage strikingly parallel occurs in the Munich Brief. "The most grave office entrusted to Us by Christ the Lord Himself, of ruling and moderating (moderandi) His Universal Church, and *feeding all His flock with the pastures of salutary doctrine.*"

of this very Encyclical. It is quite certain, then, that the Pope condemns the proposition just recited, as denying the full power given to the Roman Pontiff of inculcating true doctrine on the universal Church. But this cannot by any possibility be the case, unless the said proposition claims a wrongful exemption, not merely from the duty of obeying the Pope's commands, but also from that of believing his declarations.

Here, therefore, we will confine ourselves to this particular—the yielding interior assent to Papal judgments—and put aside for the moment that other question, which concerns obedience to Papal precepts. Pius IX., then, teaches (1) that the Pope is in the habit of putting forth certain "judgments" which "do not touch the dogmata of faith and morals," but "whose object is declared [by him] to regard the Church's rights, discipline, and general good." His declarations on his civil princedom may be given as instances in point. Pius IX. teaches (2) that interior assent cannot be refused to these judgments, "without sin and a certain sacrifice of the Catholic profession." (3) He rests this obligation of interior assent, not at all on the fact that the Pope is very much more likely to be right on such matters than a private Catholic,* but distinctly on the claim of infallibility. A moment's consideration will show this. No one doubts that the Pope claims infallibility, in exercising that power of "feeding" or teaching the universal Church, which he

We have urged in a former number (July, 1863, pp. 71-79), that under certain circumstances a certain interior assent may be reasonably claimed, for such a reason, to utterances which are not actually infallible; and we hope to pursue the same train of thought in a future article on the Pontifical Congregations.

has received from Christ.* But Pius here instructs us, that the issuing this particular class of declarations falls within that power; he instructs us, therefore, that this class of declarations is infallibly true.

Let us suppose, then, that the Catholic Episcopate, expressly or tacitly, adheres to the "Quantâ curâ:" the whole Ecclesia Docens will then claim infallibility, not for those Papal declarations only which "touch the dogmata of faith and morals," but for those also which bear on "the Church's rights, discipline, and general good." But to suppose that the Ecclesia Docens can claim an infallibility which she does not possess, is (as we have so often urged) to shake her authority to its very centre: a Catholic, who could dream of such a supposition, is already on the high road to apostasy.

One explanation more is necessary. Pius IX. supposes that such a declaration "does not touch the dogmata of faith and morals." He must mean, of course, that it does not *directly* touch them; for if it bears (as he himself expresses it) on "the Church's rights, discipline, and general good," it cannot but have an indirect connection with those dogmata.

2. No Catholic may doubt that declarations put forth by the Pontiff, in his capacity of Universal Teacher, if accepted by the Episcopate, are infallibly true; and it is the habit, therefore, of our opponents to maintain, that all those declarations of the Pope, which are not definitions of faith, are put forth by him,

* No one doubts, we say, that the Pope *claims* infallibility in exercising this power; though Gallicans deny that he possesses it, unless he is supported in his judgment by the general Episcopate.

not as Universal Teacher, but as a private doctor. The present Encyclical must dispose of such a pretence for ever. We might, indeed, had the thought occurred to us, have exposed its fallacy, when discussing the "Mirari vos" in our last number. That pronouncement was assuredly no definition of faith; yet in a subsequent Encyclical ("Singulari nos," July 10, 1834), Gregory informs the bishops that on that earlier occasion he had declared true doctrine *to the whole Catholic flock* (and here again, observe, is the same illustration to which the word "pascendi" refers), *according to the function of his office.** In regard, however, to the "Quantâ curâ," there is no need of consulting any other declaration, to understand its claim and bearing: it speaks for itself. The Pope, as already quoted, "wills and commands" that the errors censured in it "be thoroughly held *by all children of the Catholic Church*, as reprobated, proscribed, and condemned." If our opponents can argue that he says this as a private doctor, and not as Universal Teacher, they must have forgotten the meaning of words. Still more emphatically in the Syllabus, he teaches that "*all Catholics ought most firmly to hold*" that doctrine, which he had delivered on his civil princedom. When he is instructing "all Catholics" what doctrine they are "most firmly to hold," in what imaginable capacity can he be speaking, except in that of Universal Teacher?

3. We asumed in our January article (p. 42) that

* Encyclicis nostris literis datis die 15 Augusti, anni 1832; quibus sanam et quam sequi unicè fas sit doctrinam, de propositis ibidem capitibus, pro nostri officii munere Catholico gregi universo denunciavimus.

there are certain declarations of the Pope which are not in form addressed to the Universal Church, but which nevertheless are "intended for publication (as is shown by the circumstances of the case), with the purpose of inculcating some doctrine on the whole Church as theologically certain, or of denouncing some tenet to the whole Church as theologically unsound:" and to such declarations we ascribed infallibility. The reader has just seen that these two Encyclicals are exactly cases in point. But since our opponents are often extremely reluctant to believe more than actual necessity requires, it is imaginable (though we are not aware it has ever been attempted) that they may draw a distinction between Encyclicals and other pronouncements. "The former," they may say, "as being addressed to the whole Episcopate, are in some sense addressed to the Universal Church; but a Consistorial Allocution, or a letter to some individual pastor, can never be intended to inculcate Catholic doctrine on the whole body of the faithful." All such evasions are precluded by this glorious Encyclical. "Scarcely had we been elevated to this Chair of Peter," says Pius IX., "when . . . we raised our voice, and in many published *Encyclical Letters, Allocutions delivered in Consistory, and other Apostolic Letters*, we condemned the chief errors of this our most unhappy age . . . and *admonished . . . all children of the Catholic Church* that they should abhor" the pestilence. He places in one class Encyclicals, Allocutions, and other Apostolic Letters; he unites them in the common category of "having been published by him;" and he says expressly that they were directed as warnings to "*all children of the Catholic Church.*" Further, we find from the Syllabus,* that among these warnings thus put forth by him as Universal Teacher are included not merely Encyclicals and Allocutions, but various letters to this or that individual pastor; to the Archbishops of Munich, Cologne, and Friburg, and to the Bishop of Breslau: not to mention one (prop. lxxiii.) which took the form of a letter to that spiritual rebel, the King of Sardinia.

4. In the same article (p. 38) we maintained that there are various facts, over and above those recorded in Scripture, on which the Church can infallibly pronounce, in consequence of their relation with dogma. Examples of this are props. lxxii., lxxvi., lxxvii., lxxix. Our doctrine, then, on this head, has received the Pope's direct sanction.

5. Lastly, a flood of light has been thrown on the truth of that doctrine, which we maintained in our last number, by the mode in which this Papal utterance has been received throughout the Catholic world. We wish that space permitted doing justice to this theme; but we will give at least some indication of our meaning, by a few specimens of the language held by French bishops. Thus the illustrious Mgr. Parisis, bishop of Arras, in a letter to M. Baroche, dated January 18:—

In the bull "Quantâ curâ" *everything is doctrinal and even dogmatic.* This being laid down, your Excellence will understand that with us dogma is not a simple opinion. . . . *it is the Divine Truth itself, sovereign, eternal, immovable as God.* . . . *You will say to me perhaps that all the condemnations pronounced* . . *are not articles of faith.* As regards some of them I admit that they are

* See on this subject Cardinal Antonelli's letter at the end of this Essay.

not so in such sense as that those who did not admit them *would be on that account formally heretical;* but not in such sense as that persons could reject them without being *guilty of great sin under the head of faith* (sans se rendre grandement coupables en matière de foi).

The Bishop of Luçon exhorts his priests "to adhere *in spirit and in heart,* after their bishop's example, to the decisions, condemnations, and instructions" therein contained. The Bishop of Beauvais "received the decisions of the supreme authority of Jesus Christ's vicar *with the most entire submission of mind and heart,*" and well knows that on this head there is no difference between his priests' opinion and his own. The Bishop of Fréjus declares that the Encyclical is "*a Rule of Faith which every Catholic is bound to accept.*" But to cite one bishop is to cite all.

We may next refer to the "sacred invitation" issued by the Cardinal Vicar of Rome, on occasion of his fixing the time for gaining the Jubilee indulgence. There is no document, not directly Papal, which can have so much weight as this in determining the true sense and authority of the Encyclical; for it is addressed to the Catholics of Pius IX.'s own diocese, by his express sanction, and under his very eye. The following passage deserves careful attention, as bearing on the theme before us. Cardinal Patrizi has been recounting generally various errors condemned in the Encyclical, and he thus proceeds:—

"The faithful, who show themselves such in word and act, recognize in the voice of the Church's visible head *the very word of God*. . . That head has authority to address the whole Church; and he who listens not to him, declares himself as no longer appertaining to the Church, as no longer making part of Christ's flock, and accordingly as no longer having a right to the eternal inheritance of Heaven."

The first sentence here quoted would suffice, indeed, to show what is otherwise indubitable; viz., that the Cardinal Vicar does not impute actual heresy, to those who withhold assent from the doctrine of the Encyclical. But his words cannot surely mean less than this:—that those who withhold such assent, act inconsistently with their Catholic profession; assume a non-Catholic position; and are accordingly (while their indocility continues) excluded from the hope of Heaven. Here, then, we have a striking illustration and interpretation of that remarkable passage, quoted by us from the Encyclical a page or two back, which condemns the non-assent to such Papal judgments, as involving "sin and a certain sacrifice (jactura) of the Catholic profession." At the same time, we would submit to competent theologians a remark in the preceding Essay, on the case of invincible ignorance in this matter. See pp. 53, 54.

Nor should we omit Cardinal Antonelli's circular to the bishops, in forwarding them the Encyclical and Syllabus. This letter, indeed, is so important in showing the precise authority of the latter, that we should be inexcusable in not presenting it to our readers. It will be found to afford another illustration of our statement (see p. 42 of this volume), that very many pronouncements of the Holy Father are really addressed to the Universal Church, and concern, therefore, the whole episcopal body, which do not in their actual form express this fact. We are obliged to translate the circular from the French translation. In that translation it runs as follows; and the first sentence, as will be seen, is taken almost verbatim from the Encyclical :—

Our Holy Father, Pius IX., Sovereign Pontiff, being profoundly anxious for the salvation of souls and for sound doctrine, has never ceased, from the commencement of his Pontificate, to proscribe and condemn the chief errors and false doctrines of our most unhappy age, by his published Encyclicals, and Consistorial Allocutions, and other Apostolic Letters. But as it may happen that all the Pontifical Acts do not reach each one of the ordinaries, the same Sovereign Pontiff has willed that a Syllabus of the same errors should be compiled, to be sent to all the bishops of the Catholic world, in order that these bishops may have before their eyes all the errors and pernicious doctrines which he has reprobated and condemned.

He has consequently charged me to take care that this Syllabus, having been printed, should be sent to your [Eminence] on this occasion, and at this time; when the same Sovereign Pontiff, from his great solicitude for the salvation and [general] good of the Catholic Church and of the whole flock divinely entrusted to him, has thought well to write another Encyclical Letter to all the Catholic bishops. Accordingly, performing, as is my duty, with all suitable zeal and submission, the commands of the said Pontiff, I send your [Eminence] the said Syllabus together with this letter.

I seize with much pleasure this occasion of expressing my sentiments of respect and devotion to your [Eminence], and of once more subscribing myself, while I humbly kiss your hands,

Your [Eminence's] most humble and devoted servant,

G. CARD. ANTONELLI.

Rome, Dec. 8, 1864.

We may lastly quote Mgr. de Ségur's little work on the Encyclical—a work which is most highly thought of by the general body of French Catholics.

The Pope being Vicar of Jesus Christ, the supreme and *infallible* teacher of the Church, ... it is evident that when he *teaches* or commands anything in an Encyclical, every Christian is bound in conscience to submit himself. . . . . "He that *believeth* shall be saved, and he that *believeth not* shall be condemned." (Pp. 4, 5.)

ESSAY V.*

THE CHURCH INFALLIBLE IN HER MAGISTERIUM.

IN order that our readers may appreciate some of our future remarks, we must once more advert to a matter, on which we have of late been laying considerable stress: we must speak once more on the fundamental erroneousness, the violently anti-Catholic character, of that opinion, which would limit the Church's and the Holy Father's infallibility to actual definitions of faith. In addition to various arguments which we have already urged on this matter, we would entreat our readers' attention to the following considerations:—

(1) F. Perrone's lectures (whatever criticism may otherwise be made on them) have beyond question a greater value than any other work that can be named, in this respect; viz., in showing what is the view of Catholic doctrine, inculcated at this moment on theological students, by the great majority of bishops

* July, 1865. From an article called "Rome, Unionism, and Indifferentism," pp. 121—132, 163—171.

throughout the world. Now in his dissertation on the Church, he lays down a certain elementary doctrine on infallibility, as "held by Catholics and denied by all others." He does not speak of it as of one Catholic view among many, but as of the one Catholic doctrine; nor does he so much as hint, that among Catholics any other can possibly exist. We cannot better express this doctrine than in his own words:—

While the Church fulfils the office of teaching, she performs a threefold duty; viz., that of witness, of judge, and of guide (magistræ). Of witness, in proposing those truths of the Faith which she has received from Christ; of judge, in deciding controversies which either touch the faith or have reference thereto; lastly of guide, in that daily ministry whereby *through her oral and practical teaching* (vivâ voce et praxi) she instructs the faithful in all those matters which conduce to their being trained in pure doctrine and morality, and whereby she *leads them as it were by the hand along the path of eternal salvation.* Catholics contend, all non-Catholics deny, that *Christ has endowed His Church with infallibility for performing each of these duties.*—De Locis, n. 347–8.

Now it is plain on the surface, that those who limit the Church's infallibility to her definitions of faith, admit indeed her infallibility as "testis;" and to some limited extent as "judex;" but that they deny infallibility to her altogether, in her capacity of "magistra." No such view, however, is so much as known to approved theologians. According to their unanimous teaching, the Church is infallible, not only in witnessing and in judging, but in practically guiding her children to salvation.

Now let our readers consider at their leisure—though indeed it requires very prolonged consideration to exhaust the subject—how much is implied in this pregnant statement, that the Church is infallible in her "juge magisterium." Take the obvious illustration of a parent; and suppose it were revealed to me, that my mother's guidance is infallible in every particular of moral and religious training. That I should accept with unquestioning assent the very least detail of her explicit instruction, is but a small part of my submission to her authority. I should be ever studying her whole demeanour in my regard—her acts no less than her words—in order that I may more fully apprehend her implied principles of conduct, and gather those lessons of profound wisdom which she is privileged to dispense. Perhaps indeed at the present time no more important contribution could be made to scientific theology, than a full exposition of the Church's infallible "magisterium;" so that this great doctrine may be cleared of possible misconception, and vindicated against plausible objection.

(2.) This infallibility of the Church's "magisterium" is also testified by the "sensus fidelium." He who holds that the Church is infallible only in her definitions of faith, studies divine truth by a method which we must maintain to be characteristically Protestant. He takes for his principles these definitions (as contained *e. g.* in Denzinger's small volume) and manipulates them according to his own private views of history and logic, with no further deference or submission to the living Church. Now such an extravagance as this is by absolute necessity confined to highly educated intellects: the ordinary believer has no more power of proceeding by such a method, than by the more openly Protestant maxim of private judgment on Scripture. A few unsound Catholics, we repeat, may be led astray by intellectual phantoms or blinded by intellectual pride; but the great mass have imbibed one and one only method of acquiring Catholic truth. The Church, as they have been taught, in her full practical exhibition, is their one infallible guide. They well know that, if they would learn their religion, they must open their heart unreservedly to the Church's full influence; study for their guidance those manuals and spiritual books which she places in their hand; listen with docility to the instruction of her ministers; practise those duties which she prescribes in the very form in which she prescribes them; labour, in one word, that that great body of truth may sink silently and deeply into their heart, which her whole system of practice and discipline inculcates and implies.* Now it is a principle of Catholicism, that wherever the body of the faithful has unanimously imbibed one impression of fundamental doctrine, a strong presumption arises of such impression being the true one.† But even otherwise—is there any one who would openly say that there is a "royal road" to religious truth? that the highly cultivated intellect is to seek it by a method, essentially different from that accessible to the ordinary believer? that far less deference is due to the Church's practical guidance from the former than from the latter? An affirmative answer to this question is

* "As the blood flows from the heart to the body through the veins; as the vital sap insinuates itself into the whole tree, into each bough and leaf, and fibre; as water descends through a thousand channels from the mountain top to the plain; so is Christ's pure and life-giving doctrine diffused, *flowing into the whole body through a thousand organs from the Ecclesia Docens.*"—Murray, de Ecclesiâ, disp. XI., n. 15.

† *E. g.*, "In quæstione fidei communis fidelis populi sensus haud levem facit fidem."—Charmes, quoted with assent by Perrone.

involved in the opinion which we are combating; but such an answer is so obviously and monstrously anti-Catholic, that no one will venture expressly to give it. The legitimate benefit to be derived from intellectual cultivation is not (we need hardly say) that men should be less loyal and submissive to the Church; but on the contrary that their docility to her, while remaining formally the same, may become materially far greater, from the far more extensive knowledge opened to them, of her true mind, of her implied teaching, of her multifarious traditions.

(3.) According to that ultramontane doctrine which (as we shall presently urge) is alone defensible, the Pope's infallibility is precisely co-extensive with that of the Ecclesia Docens. Now if it be granted that the Pope is infallible in his constant and abiding "magisterium," in all his implied and practical teaching,—much more must he be infallible in that large body of explicit instruction, which he is constantly putting forth for the guidance of all his spiritual children. We are here referring of course, not to definitions of faith alone, but to such Papal acts as are recounted, *e. g.*, in the recent Syllabus. Acts of this kind are put forth, as the Pope himself says, in virtue of his office as Universal Teacher, and they are published for the guidance of his flock; but they vary indefinitely in the forms which they assume: sometimes they are consistorial Allocutions, sometimes Encyclicals, sometimes letters addressed to this or that individual pastor. Being intended, however, as instructions to the whole Church, it is plain that they form a part of the Holy Father's "juge magisterium;" and those who admit him to be infallible in the whole of this latter office, must admit him to be infallible inclusively in such doctrinal declarations. On the other hand, and conversely, it is hardly an exaggeration to say, that those who hold this latter infallibility, and act consistently with this belief, will be practically in the same position as if they held the former also. And at all events it is absolutely certain, as men of every party will admit, that all those who accept thoroughly either of the two above-named doctrines, will accept the other also: that all who regard the Pope as infallible in his various doctrinal declarations, will regard him as also infallible in his "juge magisterium;" and vice versâ. For all practical purposes, therefore, the question which we are now discussing is equivalent to that which we have been treating in our recent numbers, on the infallibility of those Papal declarations which are not definitions of faith.

The present, then, will be a very good opportunity, for executing a purpose which we mentioned in April; viz., the placing before our readers some sufficient sample, of the extraordinary unanimity with which the French Episcopate has recognized the infallibility of the recent Encyclical with its appended Syllabus. No errors are therein formally condemned as heretical, and against several of them no one even alleges the charge of heresy. If, therefore, the Pope is infallible in condemning them, it can only be because he is infallible in all his doctrinal declarations addressed to the whole Church, and not merely in those which are definitions of faith. Yet we shall see that the French bishops not only recognize with one voice this infallibility,—but also regard such infallibility as an elementary and familiar portion of Christian doctrine, held as a matter of course by the whole body of believers. We quote from the work named in the note;* and the peculiar importance of the point at issue will plead our excuse, if our quotations run to a considerable length.

The Bishop of Nantes:—

[The parish priests of my diocese] will not allow the faithful to forget (ignorer) *what the Catechism has taught them from their infancy,* that a doctrinal instruction emanating from the Supreme Pontiff *should be the rule of their belief* as of their moral conduct; and they will have recourse to this venerable monument [the Encyclical] *to resolve all the questions which shall be submitted to them on these subjects* (p. 107).

The Bishop of Arras:—

In the Bull "Quantâ Curâ," as in the Syllabus, everything is doctrinal and even dogmatic. . . . . For us dogma . . . is the Divine Truth itself, *eternal, sovereign, unchangeable as God;* consequently to ask of the faithful to contradict it, and of pastors to conceal it, is to ask what is impossible, *because it would be the sacrifice of eternal salvation.* . . . You will say to me perhaps . . . that all the condemnations pronounced by these two last declarations of the Holy See *are not articles of faith.* As regards some of them, I admit that they are not, in such sense that those who should not admit them would not on that account be formally heretics; but not in such sense as that [Catholics] may reject them, without becoming *greatly culpable under the head of faith.* . . . *All the bishops of France* at this day believe or profess that the Pope has received from God the special and supreme power of . . . feeding both shepherds and flocks with the bread of divine truth; because *to Peter alone and his successors it has been promised that they should never teach error* (p. 109.)

The Archbishop of Sens:—

We adhere entirely, sincerely, simply, without distinction, without reserve, to *all decrees teaching the Church's doctrine* which have been

* "L'Encyclique et les Evêques de France."

put forth since the beginning of Pius IX.'s reign. We *account it a duty* in all the faithful entrusted to our charge to adhere thereto *in spirit and in heart,* and to make thereof *the Rule of their Faith.* From whence will come to us the light which shall guide us in the midst of that thick darkness which encompasses us? It is *from the height of Peter's chair* that such light is given us *to show us our path.* Let us enter *on that path* . . . *without fear of ever losing our way.* Let us follow it with confidence; it will conduct us to salvation (p. 137).

The Archbishop of Bourges:—

Since the Church has received from our Lord the sacred deposit of doctrine, and the mission of communicating it to men with supreme and *infallible authority,* she has the right to count on her children's docile and respectful submission. Whether she exercises this power by means of general councils which the Soverign Pontiff convokes, . . . or *by dogmatic constitutions addressed from Rome to the bishops and faithful,* the obligation is always the same; for it is always the same authority which speaks—the authority of the Church; authority holy, sovereign, *infallible in doctrinal matters,* to which we all owe obedience, *unless we would renounce* (à moins de renoncer) *our title of Catholics. . . . . We adhere therefore fully and entirely to the Encyclical of Dec.* 8; we reprobate and condemn all the errors which are there reprobated and condemned, in that sense and manner in which the Pope reprobates and condemns them. . . We know but one sole *judge in faith,* but one sole doctrinal authority—the Church—the Church expressing herself *by the mouth of our revered head. . . . Rome has spoken, the cause is decided* (pp. 143, 146).

The Bishop of Puy:—

If the dogmatic and *infallible* teaching of Pius IX. contained in the Encyclical and Syllabus cannot . . . at this moment . . . be duly promulgated in ordinary form . . . *it is not the less obligatory,* the less sacred, for all; *it does not the less bind every Christian conscience;* we receive none the less, with a religious and entire submission *of spirit and heart,* all the oracles which it proclaims (p. 166)

The Bishop of Versailles:—

What must we see in the Encyclical? We must see in it condemnations pronounced *at different epochs* by an *infallible authority;*

then, theories and principles laid down by the same authority as *a basis for general instruction*. How ought we to receive the Encyclical? We should receive it as a *symbol*, as a *credo*, with *the most perfect submission* (pp. 178, 179).

The Bishop of Soissons:—

The faithful of your parishes . . . *know* that every Catholic is *obliged to adhere in conscience to the doctrinal decisions* which [the Encyclical] contains (p. 218).

The Cardinal Archbishop of Lyons:—

You have read this writing [the Encyclical] with that respect and veneration, which we owe to the words of the Vicar of Jesus Christ: you have adhered *from the bottom of your heart* to that which he teaches us: you have condemned all which he condemns, and this Encyclical will have been for you . . . *the oracle which must be listened to and believed* (p. 244).

The Archbishop of Toulouse:—

The recent documents, emanating from the authority of the Holy Apostolic See . . . contain *a doctrinal instruction;* and on matters of doctrine the Vicar of Jesus is *the first and only judge* (p. 10).

The Bishop of Nimes:—

The doctrines proclaimed by Pius IX. in the Encyclical . . . have been already promulgated more than once; the errors which he mentions have been previously condemned. Nay more, as to the eighty propositions contained in the Syllabus, the Holy Father expresses no [new] censure; he does but refer to his previous Allocutions, individual letters, or Encyclicals. All those acts which he recounts have been in our hands for a greater or less period; *the instructions which they contain under the form of dogmatic exposition or condemnation* are *accepted by the whole Church;* they have the force of law within the Church (ils y font loi); and neither the circular of your Excellence nor the decisions of the State Council can *exempt Catholics from the obligation of submitting to them*. This is an *incontestable doctrine* even according to the ancient maxims of the Gallican Church (p. 17).

The Bishop of Limoges:—

The word of Christ *speaking through the Apostolic mouth is* always faithful and worthy of all acceptation, to which word *belief is given in the heart* to justification, and confession with the mouth to salvation. The *unfailing oracle of truth* was to me a matter of greater consolation . . . . Therefore as to all the propositions censured in the aforesaid Syllabus and Encyclical, and other Apostolic Letters, I profess that all without exception are to be *rejected and condemned* in the sense and mode which the Apostolic See intends. Likewise of all the documents of the Encyclical, as far as rests with me, one iota or one point shall not pass away, but that it shall be taught and *believed* in my whole diocese (p. 19).

The Bishop of Poitiers :—

We declare that we adhere fully in spirit and in heart to all the doctrinal judgments and affirmations, to all *the rules of belief* and conduct, enunciated by our Holy Father Pius IX., *from the beginning of his Pontificate to the present day*, and we pronounce that it is *the duty of all orthodox Christians* to submit themselves to the said instructions with an humble and filial docility of their *understanding* and will (p. 31).

The Bishop of Beauvais :—

If you ask of us what line you should yourselves follow (vous devez suivre vous-mêmes), our answer will be easy. . . . In regard to doctrine, *full and perfect adhesion* of spirit and of heart to the instructions, decisions, condemnations, which emanate from the holy Roman Church, the mother and mistress of all churches (p. 38).

The Bishop of Fréjus :—

The Encyclical, which does but renew the condemnation of propositions already condemned with the unanimous consent of the Episcopate, becomes *a Rule of Faith which every Catholic is bound to accept* (pp. 55-6).

The Bishop of Saint Dié :—

[The Encyclical contains] the instructions of him "*whose faith cannot fail*," and who has been appointed to "confirm his brethren." . . . At the same to satisfy our *duty* as son and bishop of the holy Catholic Church Apostolic and Roman, surrounded in spirit by our well-beloved clergy, who, especially at this moment, make but one heart and one voice with their bishop, we *condemn all which is con-*

demned in the Encyclical of Dec. 8, 1864; we reprobate all which it reprobates, and in the sense in which it reprobates and condemns (p. 70).

The Bishop of Algiers :—

In the presence of a *dogmatic and moral bull ex cathedrâ*, emanating from him who has received of Jesus Christ the *full and entire mission of teaching the Universal Church*, the bishops could not in any manner believe themselves dispensed from *the docility of mind and heart which they owe to it* (p. 75).

The Bishop of Bayeux :—

The sentiments of profound veneration and *perfect obedience* wherewith you are animated in regard to the Sovereign Pontiff, impose on us the duty of letting you know *with what submission of spirit and heart* we have received the sacred words of the Vicar of Jesus Christ (p. 79).

The Bishop of Langres :—

Now it is in spirit and in heart, . . . *with our whole soul and without reserve, that we adhere, we and all of you with us*, to the great and salutary instructions of the Encyclical; and that we reprobate and condemn everything which the Pope reprobates and condemns, and in the same sense in which he condemns it (p. 115).

The Bishop of Gap :—

This word of the Supreme Pontiff, *of him who is "teacher of all Christians"* (Conc. Flor.) . . . has reached you by all the organs of the press. After the example of your first pastor, you will receive it with all the respect *due* to it; *with the most entire submission of mind and heart. This is an imperative and sacred duty for you and for all true Catholics* (pp. 121-2).

The Bishop of Quimper :—

[The Supreme Pontiff] is appointed by God *to direct* [men's] *conscience*. . . Far from us the thought as regards this solemn document of either adding aught to it or taking aught from it: *we adhere to it fully and without reserve* (p. 158).

The Bishop of Chartres :—

When the Church speaks, all should hear her, *if they wish still to claim the name of Catholics.* . . . We declare that the Sovereign Pontiff's letter, dated Dec. 8, prescribing the jubilee, as well as the catalogue of condemned errors annexed to it, should be the rule *which shall direct our minds and conduct* under present circumstances (p. 168).

The Bishop of Périgueux:—

We adhere emphatically (hautement), in your name as well as in our own, with submission and love to all the instructions given to the Church and the world by our Holy Father Pope Pius IX., during the whole course of his Pontificate, and particularly on that ever memorable day, Dec. 8, 1864. *We approve, affirm, and believe all which he approves, affirms, and believes; and all which he rejects, reprobates, and condemns, we reject, reprobate, and condemn.* Such is our faith, such is yours; and *with God's help it shall ever be the same as the faith of Peter's legitimate successors* (pp. 187, 188).

The Cardinal Archbishop of Chambéry:—

For many years past the venerable head of the Church has condemned some of these most dangerous errors; these condemnations have been successively published without exciting any protest. They have been recapitulated and put together in a Bull, published Dec. 8th last . . . and addressed to all the bishops of the Catholic world *that it may serve as a Rule of Belief to the faithful.* . . . It is absolutely necessary that the head of the Church may make his voice heard by his children, that he may teach them *what they must believe and practise to be saved* (pp. 191, 192).

The Bishop of Angoulême:—

The Bull Unigenitus subsists and will always subsist, venerated in the entire world as *a Rule of Faith*, from *which no one could deviate* without ceasing to be a Catholic. *It will be the same with the new Bull* (p. 201).

We have prolonged these extracts at the risk of wearying our readers, because no general account of them would suffice for the impression which we wish to convey. Some Catholics seem to think, that even if that doctrine be true which we have maintained on the infallibility of such Papal pronouncements, at least the question is an open one, and one on which good Catholics may freely take either side. But the French bishops speak of our doctrine as quite rudimental; as familiar to all Catholics; as contained in the very Catechism.*

Another inference is at once deducible from the passages which we have quoted. Benedict XIV., in his well-known letter to the supreme Inquisitor of Spain, says that the Pope's infallibility, in his teaching ex cathedrâ, is received everywhere except in France.†

---

* It is interesting to English Catholics, that their own bishops use the same explicit and unmistakable language. What can be more express than this from the Bishop of Shrewsbury?—"We cannot indeed but think that we are calling such men [those who "have presumed to question, not only the expediency, but the soundness" of the Encyclical and Syllabus] by a wrong title when we give them the name of Catholic. For does not that name imply in its essential meaning that we submit ourselves, *our views, our judgment*, on all matters of faith or morals, to the voice and decisions of the Church? . . . Nor let them pretend *with that false refinement which the spirit of insubordination suggests* to draw too nice distinctions . . . *The word that has gone forth is not the word of man, but of the Pontiff; and in that word we revere the teaching of Him by whose power it has been uttered.*"—Pastoral of April 25th. The *Church Review* of April 29, in noticing our own statements to this effect in our last number, says, "We do not so wrong the majority of our educated brethren of the Roman persuasion, as to suppose that the above *farrago of nonsense* in the least represents what they believe on the subject." The writer shows by this tone that he wishes to use conciliatory language, towards the general body of English Catholics; and he thinks he shall best accomplish that purpose, by calling the judgment of their bishops a "farrago of nonsense." *Let him name, if he can, one single Catholic bishop throughout the world, who has either stated or implied that the doctrinal decisions of the Encyclical and Syllabus are fallible.*

† Totum [Bossueti] opus versatur in asserendis propositionibus à

Now the extracts just given show most clearly that this exception no longer exists. The Bishop of Arras's testimony, *e.g.*, is expressed on this head, and no one has attempted to contradict it:—"All the bishops of France at this day," he says, "believe or profess that to Peter alone and his successors it has been promised that they should never teach error." The Catholic Episcopate then is now unanimous in this particular, and Gallicanism under present circumstances slays itself. If we start from the Gallican premiss, that the Bishops are infallible when united with their head;—we are led to the ultramontane conclusion, that their head is also infallible when speaking alone. Never had ultramontanes so much right to say (and we do most confidently say it) that theirs is the only doctrine consistently tenable by a Catholic.

(4.) The French bishops teach, then, that the Holy Father is infallible in all his doctrinal declarations, and not exclusively in his definitions of faith. That which they say on occasion of the Encyclical, he had already said in the Encyclical itself. We showed this in our last number (pp. 70-73 of this volume). He teaches therein that the Pope is in the habit of putting forth certain "judgments," which "do not touch the dogmata of faith and morals," and which assuredly, therefore, are not definitions of faith. He teaches, further, that the Pope is infallible in these judgments; and that

---

Clero Gallicano firmatis in conventu anno 1682. Difficile profectò est aliud opus reperire, quod æquè adversetur *doctrinæ extra Galliam ubique receptæ, de Summi Pontificis ex cathedrâ definientis infallibilitate ;* de ejus excellentiâ supra quodcunque concilium œcumenicum ; de ejus jure indirecto, si potissimùm religionis et Ecclesiæ commodum id exigat, super juribus temporalibus principum supremorum.

interior assent cannot be refused to them, "without sin," and without a certain "sacrifice of the Catholic profession." Every one at all acquainted with theological language will admit, that "sin" here means "mortal sin;" but all possible doubt on the subject must be removed, by the "sacred invitation" which the Cardinal Vicar of Rome issued under the Pope's own eyes, as a pastoral instruction to the Pope's own diocese. For Cardinal Patrizi says expressly that the Encyclical and Syllabus are to be received "as the very word of God;" and that he who "listens not" to the Pope so speaking, has "no longer a right to the eternal inheritance of Heaven (see p. 77-8 of this volume).

From these various considerations then (to which very many others might easily be added), we unhesitatingly draw our conclusion. Hardly any doctrine, which is not explicitly de fide, is more irrefragably certain, than that the Pope's infallibility is not confined to his definitions of faith, but that it extends over his whole practical "magisterium;" and inclusively, therefore, to all those declarations which he authoritatively puts forth, for the instruction of the Universal Church.

As we have often to speak of the Unionists, it will be desirable, before quitting this part of our subject, to consider an allegation which is frequently in their mouth. They love to speak of the great evils which have accrued to the Church, from the separation of England, *e. g.*, and to so large an extent of Germany, from the Roman See. Now as to the great majority of Unionists—those who are non-Catholic—they may most consistently say this : for they believe that the Church has been actually divided. If the Church could be divided at all, it would be impossible (no doubt) to exaggerate the calamitousness of such an event. But the question which we wish to consider concerns Catholics. How far and in what sense can Catholics truly say that the Church has suffered injury, through the lamentable defection which has taken place from her body?

Firstly, of course, the loss of so many souls, which might have been saved within visible unity, but which will not in fact be saved externally to that unity, is a grievous injury to the Church's interests: for her highest interest is the salvation of souls.

Then, further, an active intellectual process has been exercised within the Church from the first, on the Deposit of Faith. Great thinkers have busied themselves in every age, whether with analysing some individual doctrine; or harmonizing various doctrines in their mutual relation; or carrying them forward to their legitimate conclusions, theological and philosophical; or penetrating the depths of Scripture; or exploring the treasures of tradition. All this has been done under the vigilant supervision of the Holy See; which has carefully guarded the purity of this doctrinal development, and provided against the danger of unsound opinions taking root within the Church. Now the intellectual labour, of which we have spoken, has conferred inestimable services; and at no period has it been more needed than in the three last centuries. It has no doubt, therefore, inflicted very serious injury on the Church, that men of genius and learning, who (had they been Catholics) might have taken a prominent part in the work, have wasted or worse than wasted their power, by devoting it to the service of a false religion. Germans, *e. g.* (whatever their intellectual faults) are perhaps exceeded by none in critical acumen, and again in philosophical profundity. The Church then has sustained a severe detriment, from so many Germans being Protestant ; in that she has lost the benefit of such important services as they might have rendered her.

The Church then, we say, has been negatively a great sufferer by the Protestant apostasy; but no good Catholic can admit that she has positively suffered thereby. It is necessary to insist on this, because we are inclined to fear that, through confusion of thought, much unsound speculation has found access to the mind of certain Catholics. It has been implied in fact —unless we misunderstand the meaning of various expressions which have been used—that she has actually suffered in the purity of her teaching, through the defection of Protestant England and Germany; that Rome's authoritative lessons (apart of course from definitions of faith) are less simply orthodox in tendency, than they would have been had all Europe remained Catholic. Such a notion simply inverts the Church's whole constitution. God teaches the Holy See, and the Holy See teaches the Church ; it is Peter whose faith fails not, and who in his turn confirms his brethren : whereas, according to the above notion, he would not be simply the Church's teacher, but in part her disciple. Rome, let it never be forgotten, is commissioned to teach England and Germany, not England or Germany to teach Rome. So far as any Englishmen or Germans are at variance with what is authoritatively inculcated in Rome, they are infallibly in error. Rome no doubt may often wish to correct her impressions of *fact* by special communication, *e. g.*, with England; but she cannot, without abandoning her essential claims, seek correction from any source, on matters of doctrine or of principle.*

We have spoken of the Church's infallibility in her "juge magisterium." The great importance of this doctrine will be more and more evident, in proportion as we more sedulously ponder its meaning and its drift. We will here proceed to consider it under one of its many aspects; and will make a few preliminary remarks, that our meaning may be intelligible.

We will begin, then, with reciting some principal doctrines and authorized usages, tending most powerfully to influence the interior character, which are integral portions of the Catholic religion, and to which all Protestants are more or less strangers; and we will afterwards draw various inferences from this enumeration. Moreover, as we must carefully consult for brevity, we will not consider the case of Photians and other Eastern heretics or schismatics; but only of

* "This Roman chair of the most blessed Peter, which, being the mother and guide (*magistra*) of all Churches, has always preserved *whole and inviolate* the faith delivered by Christ the Lord, and faithfully taught it, showing to all men the path of salvation and *the doctrine of uncorrupted truth* . . . Where Peter is, there is the Church; and Peter, through the Roman pontiff, *furnishes truth of doctrine* (præstat fidei veritatem) *to them that seek it.*"—(Encyclical "Qui Pluribus.") "In which [Roman Church] always remains the infallible *magisterium* of the faith, and in which, therefore, apostolic tradition has ever been preserved."—(Encyclical "Nostis et nobiscum.") "In which [Roman Church] *alone* religion has been inviolably preserved, and *from which all other Churches must borrow the tradition of faith.*"—(Bull "Ineffabilis.")

European Protestants and English Tractarians. Lastly, we confine our examination to matters which directly and importantly affect the interior character; there being other doctrines, truly momentous in various other respects, on which we do not touch.

(1.) Catholics practically hold, no less than speculatively believe, that He who died on the cross is the Eternal God. Putting aside the Tractarians, we believe the number of Protestants to be extremely small, who practically hold this doctrine; though the great majority of them consider themselves to believe it. And we shall see the reason of this, when we consider the principal means whereby the Catholic Church secures its true presentation to the mind of her children. We do not here speak on books of meditation, nor again of scientific theology; because these, though instruments of signal efficacy, are available, of course, only for the educated classes. Nor again do we speak of the Catechism; which is amply sufficient for engendering speculative belief in the great doctrine, but not always for ensuring its full practical apprehension. The means whereby the great body of Catholics is duly trained in this respect, seem to us mainly two; —devotion to the Blessed Sacrament, and to Our Lady: and since Protestants, in their blindness and ignorance, have abandoned both, it is no matter of surprise that the treasure has escaped from their grasp. The belief that, by a stupendous miracle, the Redeemer is personally present in every Tabernacle, impresses the mind with a sense of His indefinite greatness; while the divine worship, internal and external, which Catholics offer to the Blessed Sacrament day after day, preserves in their mind the fresh and vivid impression of His Divine Personality. Then as regards devotion to our Blessed Lady. The practice, so peculiar to Catholics, and at the same time so universal among them, of uniting themselves with Mary in the contemplation of Jesus, unspeakably elevates their conception of His Divine Majesty. Yet we cannot wonder that Protestants reprobate devotion to our Lady altogether; for their own practical conception of Christ rises hardly (if at all) above the Catholic's conception of Christ's purest creature.

(2.) Firm belief in the Real Presence, and the habit of frequent communion, as is known by all who try the experiment, produce in the mind a profound and incommunicable effect of their own.

(3.) Devotion to our Lady is the peculiar heritage of Catholics. The immense majority of Protestants regard it with reprobation and horror; those more lenient, with indulgence and excuse: but Catholics cherish it as among their dearest possessions and their highest privileges. We will here appeal to those Catholics who have once been Protestants. We will suppose them to have accepted on faith that fully-developed Marian devotion which is *there* encouraged, whither all sound believers look for light and guidance,—viz., in Rome; and we will further suppose that they have practised assiduously the devotion thus learnt. Let us even put the case that these men have been Tractarians; and therefore, even in their pre-Catholic days, have really embraced and practically apprehended the doctrine of our Lord's Divine Personality. These, however, no less than others, find that their devotion to Mary, while unspeakably intensifying their awe and reverence, has, at the same time, given a quality of tenderness, confidingness, intimacy, to their love of Him, which has been an absolutely new experience; and, generally, that it has imparted a familiarity with the invisible world, a realization of supernatural truth, an unworldliness of thought and affection, a practical belief in the efficacy of prayer, a power of self-control, to which otherwise they would have been strangers.

(4.) All Catholics recognize the Evangelical Counsels; and consider that those who follow them pursue a higher and more heavenly method of life than any other.

(5.) Consider, again, the Saints of the Church: how singularly like to each other! how singularly unlike to all besides! It is part of Catholic doctrine, that the Church is actually infallible in proposing these holy beings to the love and reverence of the faithful. Moreover the practice is earnestly inculcated on every Catholic, of studying carefully their acts and lives, as the one highest and truest exhibition of Christianity; as presenting the one type of character most acceptable to God—the type of character, by approximating to which, and in no other way, can men become better Christians.

(6.) Whether in perusing these lives, or in studying works of ascetic theology, all Catholics are taught, that the one way of rising in true holiness, is to unite diffidence in self with confidence in God; in other words, to labour energetically towards fulfilment of His Will, in the spirit of simple reliance on His strength as enabling them to do so. One school of Protestants denies this doctrine, by affirming that all our efforts for consistent obedience are vain, and, indeed, anti-Christian; and that our best acts are in God's sight but as filthy rags. The opposite school, ignoring or denying original sin, holds that we can really advance to our true end, by works done in our natural strength, and in the spirit of self-reliance.

(7.) It is an essential truth of Catholicism, that the one end for which man was created is the love and service of God; that men are more admirable, more excellent, more perfect as men, not at all in proportion as they are more intellectual, or more gifted with practical power, or more nobly descended, but exclusively as they are more morally and spiritually advanced. On no point is there more real difference than on this, between the respective morality of Catholics and Protestants.

(8.) All Catholics are required to go annually to confession; and are earnestly exhorted, both to go much oftener, and also to practise regularly and systematically a rigid examination of conscience. Moreover, in the Confessional they submit themselves to the priest, both as their judge and their physician; while he is obliged to adjust his counsels and decisions by a whole system of moral and ascetical theology, which he is authoritatively taught in his ecclesiastical education.

(9.) Catholics hold that even the smallest sin is a greater evil than any other in the world *except* sin; that for each smallest sin future suffering (in Purgatory) is justly due; that efficacious repentance for venial sin is far from easy; that men cannot in this life obtain (whether by indulgences or otherwise) remission for the punishment of any one such sin, *without* efficaciously repenting it. We are not denying that after death the penalty may be shortened, or even removed altogether, by the prayers of survivors or by the indulgences which these may gain; but still the doctrine which we have mentioned stands out in startling contrast with Protestant misbelief. Even the everlasting punishment of mortal sins is fast disappearing out of the Protestant's creed; and a Catholic's sensitiveness to small offences was always unintelligible to the Protestant world. Matt. v. 17—19 may be thought to have been specially pronounced by anticipation, against those frightful heresies introduced by Luther, which have pervaded Protestantism in all its phases like a besetting plague.

(10.) Catholics have also a very real and influential belief, in the constant battle to be waged, by those who would obtain salvation, against the attacks of those evil spirits who are so crafty and sagacious, and, at the same time, such malignant enemies to God and man. Such a belief has now hardly any practical existence with most Protestants.

(11.) An English Catholic has a very far closer corporate connection with a French or Italian Catholic, than with an English Protestant. He owes immeasurably more unreserved attachment to the Church than to the State; and holds, moreover, as of divine faith, that the Pope is by God's immediate appointment the Church's Supreme Ruler. Consequently his one reasonable attitude of mind towards the Holy Father is an immeasurably more ardent and (as it were) chivalrous loyalty, than was due, *e. g.*, to the Stuarts, even on the highest theory of divine right.

We need not continue our enumeration further; and

we are obliged to confine our remarks on it within the briefest possible space :—

I. A very little consideration will show, that a habit of pondering on those truths, and diligently practising those usages, which we have now mentioned, must necessarily engender a most peculiar and pronounced interior character — one most widely different from any other. It may be alleged, indeed, that certain extreme Tractarians, by pondering on their own doctrines, would be similarly affected; we will remark, therefore, that, though we cannot agree with this statement, its truth would in no respect affect our argument.

II. Further, God revealed Catholic doctrine for the very end that men should contemplate and dwell on it. Since, therefore, the duly pondering on Catholic doctrine leads to a certain most definite interior character, this character must be singularly pleasing to God. It cannot be saying too much, to affirm that the production of this character is one principal end for which God revealed Catholic dogma.

III. Again, as this character would infallibly be produced by the contemplation of Catholic dogma, so the converse also holds: those who possess it will understand far better than any others the true force and bearing of such dogma; and on various matters of thought will instinctively cleave to sound opinions, while they shun those which are unsound.

IV. Indeed, this interior character may be considered as substantially identical with what are called "Catholic instincts." Those who possess it have a most special gift (supposing them to possess adequate knowledge of *facts*) of seeing on each occasion which is God's Preference, and how they can best please Him. It ranks them among a Catholic's most precious possessions.

V. Here occurs a vital question. Great multitudes have really not the opportunity or the gift of contemplating Catholic doctrines one by one. Have these men no means of acquiring this most precious possession? On the contrary, God has specially provided for their need, by enjoining that duty on which we laid stress at the outset of our article; viz., docility to the Church's "juge magisterium." By unreservedly surrendering themselves to the Church's influence in every shape; by being diligent in the Catholic duties of their station; by reading those books which have the Church's sanction; by seeking the company of priests, and of those laymen who are called abroad in derision "clericals;" by avoiding familiar intimacy, whether with persons of a different religion, or with unsound and disloyal Catholics; by exercising extreme caution and reserve in all intercourse with Protestants and all study of Protestant literature;—by these and a thousand similar methods all may imbibe that true Catholic spirit, which places them in real sympathy with the Church's mind; gives them the instinctive habit of obedience to ecclesiastical authority; and constitutes them the Church's trustworthy defenders.

VI. Since the season of childhood and youth is immeasurably the most impressible of all, it is impossible to exaggerate the importance of preserving the purity of a Catholic atmosphere throughout the whole of education. Far better for Catholic youths to be in constant contact with men sick of the plague, than with men aliens to the Church.

VII. Even intellectually speaking, no result can be more contemptible than that which ensues on mixed education. There is no surer mark of an uneducated and uncultivated mind, than that a man's practical judgment on facts as they occur, shall be at variance with the theoretical principles which he speculatively accepts. Suppose, *e. g.*, a politician, who is busy in forwarding measures, condemned by that theory on political economy which he professes to accept. What would result? We should all cry out against his shallowness, and lament that he had received no better intellectual training. Now, this is the necessary result of mixed education. The unhappy Catholic who (whether from his own fault or that of others) is so disadvantageously circumstanced, becomes a contemptible mongrel: Catholic in his speculative convictions, non-Catholic in his practical judgments; holding one doctrine as an universal truth, and a doctrine precisely contradictory on almost every particular which that universal truth comprises.

VIII. Further, we can thus discern (see prop. lxxix. of the Syllabus) the deplorable nature of that calamity which overspread Europe, when unhappy circumstances necessitated, in so many countries, the civil toleration of religious error. The Catholic atmosphere, instead of pervading the nation, is withdrawn, as it were, within the more purely ecclesiastical sphere; a wide and ever increasing gulf opens between the clergy on one hand, and the great body of the laity on the other; religious indifferentism eats like a cancer into the very vitals of society; a disease, perhaps, by the very reason of its impalpableness and subtlety, more perilous than almost any other by which the body politic can be affected.

IX. Lastly, as has been more than once implied, fraternization and familiar intercourse, whether with Protestants or with unsound and disloyal Catholics, tends inevitably to destroy, not indeed all speculative belief, but at least all practical apprehension, of those great truths which Christ came to teach us.

Now, men of all parties will agree that the principles here stated, if true, give abundant reason for the detestation and abhorrence which we feel for indifferentism, whether Unionistic or Protestant.

The Catholic's answer to them both is most simple. Either Christ did, or did not, commit a large body of momentous dogma to the infallible guardianship of the Holy See and the Catholic Episcopate. To believe that He did not, is to abandon Catholicism. If He did—as every Catholic is required to believe that He did—Catholics have nothing for it but to accept with humble submission that body of dogma, precisely as it is taught them by that authority which Christ has empowered infallibly to propose it. We do not deny that there are many open questions; that various tenets, held firmly by individual Catholics, are, nevertheless, in no sense obligatory on a Catholic's belief; but we must maintain that no private Catholic can even guess, by his own judgment, what questions are or are not open. The good Catholic submits his judgment unreservedly to the Holy See; he holds those tenets to be respectively heretical, unsound, improbable, which the Holy Father declares to be such; he thinks independently for himself on those questions alone, which the Holy Father leaves perfectly free.

It is urged by many, as an argument against denunciation of unsound Catholics, that members of the Church should at least live in union with each other, if they would succeed in their aggression on the world.

No end, we reply, can be more inestimably important, than that sound and loyal Catholics—those heartily submissive both in intellect and will to the Holy See—should be bound together in firmest union. But are all Catholics such? Certain persons will reject, indeed, any tenet as *heretical* which the Church so denounces, but will not ascribe to a proposition, as infallibly deserved, any *lesser* censure with which the Church may have branded it: nor will they accept as infallibly true those instructions of the Holy Father (such as the "Mirari vos," or the "Quantâ curâ" with its appended Syllabus) which are not definitions of faith. These men do not, therefore, actually cease to be Catholics, but they are unsound and disloyal Catholics; and they commit, moreover, as we must maintain, (materially at least) mortal sin. So far from its being desirable that a private Catholic should be in "union" with such men, his attitude of mind should be simply antagonistic to their whole position; he should regard them as mischievous and dangerous rebels. Certainly he should tenderly love them, as he should tenderly love heretics and schismatics. Certainly he should dwell admiringly on their good qualities, and give their every act the most favourable interpretation of which it is reasonably susceptible: but this again is also his duty towards heretics and schismatics. And his love for one class, as for the other, should be exhibited, not by fraternizing with them (God forbid !), but by endeavouring (if he have the opportunity) to awaken in them a sense of their error and peril. Unionists show no great "union" of heart with Ultramontanes; and indifferentists in general quite forget their philosophical indifference, where Ultramontanism is in question. We may be permitted, we suppose, to abhor the principles of both classes, as cordially as they abhor ours.

The great mass of Catholics, as we observed at the outset of this article, have no such intellectual cultivation, as to be tempted towards that miserable disloyalty to the Holy See of which we have just spoken. And among educated Catholics there is a large and (we really believe) an increasing class, who look to Rome as to their one guiding star amid the tempests of life; who obey her every command and wish; who are docile, not merely to her smallest expressed instructions, but to her whole practical "magisterium." That these men may come more and more to know each other, to understand each other, to love each other; that those otherwise minded may be led in ever increasing numbers to see the error of their ways; that such loyal and devoted subjects may form an impregnable barrier of defence to the Holy See; that through their co-operation the Chair of Peter may be, in a constantly increasing degree, revered through the world as the one Chair of Truth, and as the highest seat of legitimate authority;—this is a wish and prayer for Christain "union," which we express with deep sincerity and from the bottom of our heart. Such is that "union," which alone is healthy and stable, because it is based on the principle of submission. Let those who desire union remember, that the Holy See has been established by Christ as the one bond and means of unity.

ESSAY VI.*

DR. MURRAY'S TESTIMONY.

DR. MURRAY'S disputation,† on the "object" of the Church's authority, is to our mind both the ablest and the most original of all. When we say "original," we do not mean, of course, that its teaching is new, for so it must be erroneous; but that the author has here most effectively marshalled and arranged various matters of doctrine, which had never hitherto been contemplated under one point of view; and that he has supported the received truths by a most admirable collection of arguments.

By the "object" of the Church's authority, he means the range over which her infallible authority extends. He assumes, of course, from the earlier part of his treatise, that she is infallible in those doctrines which are actually of faith; and he proceeds to the other objects of her infallibility. Firstly (p. 203), she is infallible in determining "Catholic truths;" *i.e.*, truths which she pronounces to be in such sense indissolubly bound up with the Faith, that

* July, 1865. From "Notices of Books," pp. 262, 263.

† "Tractatus de Ecclesiâ Christi, tom. iii., fasc. 1."

their contradictories (if not heretical) are theologically unsound and censurable. This is the thesis which we have of late been earnestly enforcing in this REVIEW; and Dr. Murray tells us that we are supported by every approved theologian without exception (p. 240). He mentions, in fact, only three theologians as opposed to it: Holden, whose unsoundness is notorious; Chrismann, a pupil of Dr. Döllinger's; and Muratori. Our own thesis is considered by Dr. Murray to be immediately "revealed and definable as of Catholic faith" (p. 226). He gives four reasons for this conclusion, for the full exposition of which we must refer to his volume (pp. 236—240). (1.) If the Church were not infallible in such determinations, she would often by her authoritative action betray the Faith instead of defending it. (2.) The Church condemns propositions, or teaches their contradictory, in her character of "magistra;" but in that character she is infallible. (3.) She often puts forth these lesser censures, with the same formality and unhesitating confidence, with which she pronounces a condemnation of heresy. (4.) Not so much as a hint is to be found in the Fathers or in the theological schools, that the Church can possibly teach anything with a fallible authority. The author proceeds to answer the various objections which have been made to his doctrine; an easy task, for they are incredibly weak.

Secondly (p. 247), he discusses the Church's infallibility in her moral judgments, general and particular. The latter case presents some difficulty, and we would refer to an admirable remark in n. 83 (p. 250).

Thirdly, in her disciplinary enactments (p. 250). It is well known that the Church is infallible in matters of universal discipline; *i.e.*, that she is not permittted to enact laws, which cannot be obeyed consistently with sound doctrine and morality.

Fourthly, on dogmatical facts (p. 256). We believe that in no previous treatise has this very momentous question been at all so completely treated. Dr. Murray gives the best definition we have ever seen of a "dogmatical fact," and enumerates successively the following different instances:—(1.) That such or such a Pontiff—say Gregory XVI.—was truly Pope; (2.) that such or such a Council was Ecumenical; (3.) that such or such a theological expression—say "transubstantiation"—is accurate and apposite; (4.) that such or such a book contains sound or unsound doctrine, or that it contains such or such a doctrine in particular; (5.) that such or such a system of education is safe or pernicious; (6.) that such or such a society—say the Freemasons—is safe or dangerous intrinsically or extrinsically; (7.) that such or such a person is really a Saint [or, in other words, the Church is infallible in canonization]; (8.) that such or such a religious order is good and useful. Over all these dogmatical facts extends the Church's infallible authority.

Fifthly, our author treats on the Church's infallibility within the sphere of philosophy (p. 323); a question so important in these days of intellectual revolt. Under this head occurs a full discussion of Galileo's case (pp. 336—343), of which we hope to make much use in our own treatment of the same subject.

ESSAY VII.*

DOCTRINAL DECREES OF A PONTIFICAL CONGREGATION.

"I HOLD firmly every doctrine defined by the Church "as of faith, and am therefore as fully a Catholic "as any one can be. Moreover, before I submitted "to the Church, I had understood that all Catholics "admit the maxim, 'in necessary things, unity; in "doubtful things, liberty; in all things, charity.' I "have therefore extremely strong ground of complaint. "For whereas all tenets undefined by the Church are "emphatically 'dubia,' my 'liberty' in their regard is "seriously hampered, by the busy intermeddling of "certain Pontifical Congregations, for which no one "claims infallibility. Take one instance out of a "thousand. I have full right, as a Catholic, to hold "that the Pope's civil princedom is injurious to true "religion. Yet if I publish this opinion, my book is "put on the Index; nay, if I am even known to hold "it, I am regarded by my brother Catholics with deep "suspicion and alienation. Many of my friends assure "me further, and I suppose correctly, that a doctrinal "decree of these Congregations imposes on me an

* October, 1865. From an article called "Doctrinal Decrees of a Pontifical Congregation.—The Case of Galileo," pp. 376—425.

"obligation of silence; though how the Church can "be defended for silencing that which at last may turn "out to be the truth, no one has attempted to explain. "These tactics will, no doubt, seriously injure the cause "to which I adhere; yet ultimately that cause, as being "true, will prevail. Whenever it does prevail—when "all Catholics have come to embrace that very tenet "which they now denounce—the Church's command "of silence will be tacitly withdrawn and smuggled "out of sight; and Catholic controversialists will be "eager in pointing out, that no one ever claimed in-"fallibility for the mere decree of a Congregation. "But I will venture to predict, that neither those con-"troversialists, nor yet the ecclesiastical authorities, "will frankly express shame, or even regret, for that "most unwarrantable interference with Catholic liberty "of which the latter have been guilty; and which has "so grievously retarded the triumph of truth. Or "rather, why do I speak of the future, when we see "the future in the past and present? These fallible "but formidable Congregations condemned as heretical "in his time that very Galileo, whom the Pope him-"self now admits to have taught truly. The Church "did all she could to retain men in the darkness of "Geocentricism; and at this very day seems to have "learned no wisdom at all, from the disastrous conse-"quences of her former usurpation.

"This case of Galileo, indeed, cannot be too con-"stantly kept in view, as a *reductio ad absurdum* of "various ultramontane notions; notions which are "still expressed as confidently (I may say as shame-"lessly) as though Galileo's condemnation were not "an established fact. We are told, forsooth, that a "sound and loyal Catholic tries to be in harmony with "the spirit of Rome, and to follow every indication of "the Church's mind. Now if any utterance in the "world can justly be taken as an exponent of the "Church's mind, as an indication of the spirit of "Rome, it is the solemn decree of a Pontifical Con-"gregation, sanctioned and approved by the Pope "himself. It would appear, then, that for the space "of almost one hundred and fifty years, every sound "and loyal Catholic would have opposed, on theological "grounds, all scientific advocacy of the earth's motion. "A good Catholic of 1865 is to be in direct theological "opposition with a good Catholic of 1616. Then, "again, Pope Zachary condemned all belief in the "antipodes; and an ultramontane therefore of the "time would have followed him in his absurdity."

Those who have been at all familiar with the *Home and Foreign Review* and with the later numbers of the *Rambler*, will admit that we have here accurately expressed a line of argument, which was constantly recurring in their pages. Nor must we imitate the proverbial ostrich; and suppose that, because these reviews have ceased to exist, the school which animated them has ceased to think. There is no inconsiderable number, we fear, of educated Catholics, both here and abroad, who more or less fully sympathize with the view of things which we have just drawn out; and those therefore who believe more soundly, must not shrink from encountering it, unless they would abandon altogether the field of reasoning. It is true, no doubt, that moral faults—pride, intellectualism, worldliness—are greatly at the root of all this disaffection, in the case of many who have imbibed the poison; but as in the more extreme case of heretics a similar fact does not abrogate the obligation of controversy, so neither in the instance before us. No doubt it rarely happens, that controversy produces at the moment any sensible effect; yet in the long run it tells and has its weight. Accordingly, in our three last numbers, we have been preparing our way for a full reply to this line of objection; and we hope in our present article satisfactorily to conclude our argument.

Now firstly and chiefly, the foregoing effusion most singularly omits all reference to what is really the one critical point. It is persistently implied by these unsound Catholics, that there are but two kinds of ecclesiastical pronouncement to be taken into account: on the one hand, those definitions of faith, which every Catholic admits to be infallible; and on the other hand, those congregational decrees, for which no one claims that attribute. But the fact really is, that the whole question turns practically on a class of declarations which is intermediate between the two, and which (of late years at least) has been far larger in extent than either. We refer to those doctrinal instructions, which are not indeed definitions of faith, but which nevertheless are put forth, not by Congregations, but by the Pope himself as Universal Teacher; instructions which condemn every contradictory tenet, not as heretical, but as deserving some lesser theological censure. Now the various tenets to which our opponents are principally wedded, are condemned, not primarily by the Congregations, but by the Pope himself, thus speaking ex cathedrâ. That doctrine, *e. g.*, on his civil princedom, which good Catholics maintain, has been taught by him in several of these utterances;

and the Syllabus recites them all for our guidance. Those tenets again which claim for secular science entire exemption from ecclesiastical control, were not censured by a Congregation, but by the Fröhschammer and Munich briefs. Then the condemnation of Hermes and of Günther, which have closed to Catholics so large a number of philosophical questions, proceeded directly from Gregory XVI. and Pius IX. respectively. If such Papal pronouncements—accepted as they always are by the whole Episcopate—were not infallible, our mouth would be closed; we should find it impossible to deny, both that our opponents are most harshly treated, and that the interests of truth are indefensibly violated. It is on this account that we have argued so earnestly in recent numbers, both from authority and from theological reason, that these pronouncements are beyond all possible question infallible; and that no Catholic is at liberty, under pain of (materially, at least, committing) mortal sin, to doubt their truth. Our arguments are before the world. If our opponents reply to them, we will carefully consider and examine every such reply; but if they decline doing so, let them not complain (as they are somewhat fond of complaining) that they are censured but not answered.

However, it is but reasonable to admit that arguments retain their own objective force, and are not refuted by its being shown that they do not benefit the party adducing them. Moreover, the objections to Catholic truth, founded on Galileo's condemnation, are at first sight so plausible, that there is no anti-Catholic reasoning in the world which more imperatively demands an answer. "How could it be legitimate to claim interior assent for a decision, which was confessedly fallible; and which, in fact, as all the world now admits, was grievously erroneous?" "How can it be always the more perfect course to follow the Church's spirit and guidance? since those who did so in the seventeenth century rejected as heretical that which all Catholics now admit to be true." In the next Essay we will enter fully and unreservedly on this case, and vindicate everything which the Roman Congregations did. We may, therefore, reasonably claim from our readers that our discussion on the general question—on the doctrinal decrees of a Pontifical Congregation—be not frustrated from its due effect on their mind, through their preconceived impression on this particular case of the Florentine astronomer.

On the Pontifical Congregations, full information will be found in Bouix's volume "de Curià Romanâ"; which we cannot too warmly recommend to those interested in such matters. We are here, however, only concerned with two; viz., those of the Inquisition and the Index: nor even with these, save as regards the doctrinal decrees which they issue from time to time.* Does any theologian claim infallibility for these? By infallibility is meant, not the mere fact of inerrancy, but the Divine promise of inerrability; and this being supposed, we reply that infallibility is not ascribed to these decrees, merely as such, even by their most earnest upholders. Bouix expresses very clearly the

* It can hardly be necessary to explain that a "doctrinal" decree is one, the main purport of which is not to command or to prohibit, but to declare that this or that proposition is theologically sound or erroneous.

reason for such non-ascription. Whatever authority these Congregations possess, is delegated to them by the Supreme Pontiff; and he can delegate indeed his jurisdiction, but not his infallibility (p. 475).

Under these circumstances some Catholics, if we rightly understand them, have maintained that every doctrinal decree of either Congregation is purely disciplinary; that it is not intended by the Pope to have any other effect, than to forbid all public advocacy of the censured tenet; and that the yielding to it interior assent, is neither commanded, nor even counselled. But such an opinion cannot be maintained for a moment. In the case of Galileo, it is patent on the surface that interior assent was required, both by Paul V. and by Urban VIII, to a doctrinal decree of the Index. But without dwelling on one particular case, consider this general fact:—It is a constant practice with the Congregation of the Index to say expressly of a condemned author, where it can be said with truth, "he laudably submitted himself" to the condemnation; and it is well known by all acquainted with facts, that the mere promise of silence will never suffice to obtain this eulogy. It is "laudable," therefore, that a Catholic writer, when condemned, shall assent to the justice of his condemnation; and far more certainly, therefore, must the Holy Father account it laudable, that every Catholic shall yield interior assent to a formal decree on doctrine, which the Congregation may put forth expressly and deliberately. Indeed, it is clear that (at all events), since the recent Encyclical and Syllabus, no Catholic is permitted to hold the opinion which we combat; for the recent Encyclical and Syllabus make it absolutely certain, that the Munich Brief was a dogmatic decision pronounced ex cathedrâ and consequently infallible. But the Munich Brief rules as follows :—

And we also persuade ourselves, that these men did not intend to declare that *that perfect adhesion towards revealed truths*, which they acknowledged to be altogether necessary for obtaining true scientific progress and for confuting error, can be obtained, if faith and obedience be only rendered to dogmata expressly defined by the Church. For, even if the question were concerning that subjection which is to be rendered by an act of divine faith, such subjection should not be limited, &c. &c. . . . But . . . the men of this Congress should admit, that it is not enough for Catholic men of science to receive and venerate the above-named dogmata of the Church ; but that it is also necessary that they submit themselves, as well to *the doctrinal decisions which are put forth by the Pontifical Congregations*, as also to those heads of doctrine, &c.

Now, it is very plain that throughout this passage the question is not of "respectful silence," but of interior assent. It refers at starting to the due means of securing "perfect adhesion to revealed truths;" *i.e.*, of course, true and interior adhesion to them. Moreover, the Pope claims submission in one sentence (1) to these decrees, and (2) to those heads of doctrine recognized as absolutely certain "by the common and consistent agreement of Catholics." Now, no one will doubt that the "submission" claimed for the latter is interior assent; hence the submission claimed for the former is interior assent also.

Here, then, we are in direct contact with the central difficulty of the question: the claim of interior assent to fallible decrees. Yet, before grappling with this difficulty, we must enter on one further inquiry. We have said that no doctrinal pronouncement of a Congregation is infallible "merely as such;" but can it ever happen that what, in form, is the doctrinal pronouncement of a Congregation, is, in fact, an utterance ex cathedrâ of the Supreme Pontiff? We shall approach this necessary inquiry at greater advantage, if we first complete in one particular that doctrine which we have been recently advocating, on the Pope's immediate doctrinal instructions. In our January number we thus expressed ourselves :—

> Let us suppose the Pope to put out some declaration, which, whatever its form, is intended for publication (as is shown by the circumstances of the case), with the purpose of inculcating some doctrine on the whole Church as theologically certain, or of denouncing some tenet to the whole Church as theologically unsound. . . . We maintain that the doctrine so inculcated is infallibly true; and that the tenet so denounced infallibly merits that particular censure which has been expressed; and that the contrary opinion is theologically unsound (p. 42 of this volume).

The question has been asked, how, in the case of any given Papal document, we can be certain that such is its purpose. Several declarations for which we claim infallibility are, in form, addresses to some individual pastor; and it may be even said that, in a later passage; we made an admission which throws obscurity over the whole subject. "The Pope," we said, "may give some doctrinal decision as head of the Church, and yet not as Universal Teacher. Some individual may ask at his hands, and receive, practical direction on the doctrine to be followed in a particular case, while yet the Pope has no thought at all of determining the question for the whole Church and for all time" (p. 50). How can we possibly tell, inquires the objector, whether a letter to the Archbishop of Cologne or of Munich is intended as a doctrinal instruction for the whole Church, or merely as a practical direction to that particular prelate? The question demands an answer, and we had purposely reserved our answer to this very place.

(1) The great majority of these infallible declarations are *not* addressed to any individual pastor or section of the Church: they are contained in Allocutions, Encyclicals, or other Apostolic Letters, which have not even the appearance of being intended for one Catholic rather than for another. In none of these cases does the difficulty arise. Whatever doctrinal declaration is contained in any one of these, is pronounced ex cathedrâ and infallibly.

(2) We must suppose that the inquirer is really docile, and desirous of imbibing the full lesson of doctrine which the Church dispenses. Several unsound Catholics seem to regard the infallible knowledge of truth, not as an inappreciable blessing, but as an almost intolerable burden. For such men we are not writing. If they choose to shut their eyes, it is their own fault that they lose their way. It is quite impossible, in their state of mind, that they can hold any Catholic truth Catholically, because their state of mind is essentially anti-Catholic.

(3) The Holy Father has not yet (so far as we know) expressly and clearly laid down any universal mark of distinction, between those letters, addressed in form to individual bishops, which are, and which are not, ex cathedrâ. There will, therefore, probably be some few, of which it is really uncertain whether they are actually infallible or not. We see no kind of inconvenience in this admission. Even if not infallible, they possess the very highest authority short of infalli-

bility; and no contemporary Catholic, possessing the most ordinary humility, will dream of dissenting from any doctrine which they teach.* On this head—for it is practically very important—we will repeat some remarks made in our January number :—

Meanwhile an objection has been urged against our whole view, which some thinkers regard as very serious. They consider that "the gulf is infinite which separates what is of faith from what is not of faith," and allege very truly that our theory presents Catholic doctrine in a most different aspect. To us, their objection appears as unphilosophical as it is untheological. Is it the case in secular science that a line can be broadly and sharply drawn, such that all on one side of that line is absolutely certain truth, while all on the other side is quite open and undetermined? Is not the opposite fact notorious? Some conclusions are absolutely established; others nearly so; others, again, under present circumstances, are much more probable than their contradictories, yet by no means sure not to be afterwards disproved; and so, along a kind of graduated scale, we finally arrive at those on which, as yet, one side is not more probable than the other. So in theology. One class of doctrines unquestionably demands the assent of divine faith. Of a second class, it is quite certain that they are infallibly true, and probable that they are an actual part of the deposit. A third class are beyond all doubt infallibly true, yet with no pretensions to be strictly of faith. Of a fourth class, it is more or less probable that they are infallibly true. A fifth class are almost certainly true, though not infallibly determined. And so by degrees we arrive at those, on which every well-instructed Catholic has full liberty to take one side or the other. Thus, the pursuit of theological science becomes one sustained discipline of intellectual docility; thus the student is constantly reminded, that he thinks under the assiduous superintendence and direction of that Holy See, whose continuous infallibility is the abiding light of Catholic doctrine.

---

* Our meaning in this word "contemporary" will appear at the end of the next Essay.

(4) The question, in regard to any given Papal letter, is simply this. Are the doctrinal declarations which it may contain intended as authoritative and final determinations for the whole Church? Or are they intended, on the other hand, as mere practical directions to the individual addressed, as to the doctrine which he is to follow in a particular case? Now, in the large majority of instances, a study of the document itself will show most unmistakably to which class it belongs. We should be glad, did our limits permit, to examine several in this respect; but we must confine ourselves to one of each kind.

As our instance of the former class, we will take Pius IX.'s letter to the Archbishop of Cologne condemning Günther: "Eximiam tuam," June 15, 1857. We now, indeed, know for certain, from the Syllabus, that Pius IX. did intend this as an infallible instruction; but we must maintain that even otherwise its internal evidence sufficed to render this fact indubitable. The Holy Father begins by referring to "the duty of his apostolic ministry," and the extreme importance of "preserving entire and inviolate the Deposit of Faith" wherewith he is intrusted. When he heard, therefore, he adds, that many propositions of Günther were theologically unsound, he at once commanded the Congregation of the Index to examine carefully all that philosopher's works, and report to him the result. This, therefore, the Congregation did; it found in those works a large mass of error; and put forth a decree condemning and interdicting them. This decree, says the Holy Father, "sanctioned as it was by our authority, and published by our command," was sufficient to let *all Catholics* know that Günther's doctrine "might not be regarded as sound." Certain persons, however, the Pontiff implies, fancied that this decree did not carry with it full weight, because it did not note any definite propositions of Günther, nor express any special and determinate censure. These persons, he declares, are quite mistaken in thinking so lightly of the decree; and they are also extremely in error, if they think there were no definite propositions which the Congregation found censurable. Pius IX. then proceeds to the main doctrinal content of his letter, and specifies various deplorable errors advocated by Günther. Now we will not say merely that no candid person,—but that no person, however uncandid, possessing ordinary common sense,—would account this letter as merely intended for giving doctrinal directions to a particular bishop. Its purport is this: that all Catholics were bound, before he issued it, to repudiate Günther's tenets; but that as some difficulty had been felt from the non-enumeration of special errors, such enumeration he here gives. The whole doctrinal portion of the letter bears on this one question, what *all Catholics* are required to hold and to reject.

With this letter let us contrast, as our instance of the other class, Pope Zachary's letter to St. Boniface, in which the antipodes are mentioned. In the next Essay we will show that no false doctrine at all is upholden in this letter; but it will show the unscrupulous carelessness with which anti-catholic controversy is often carried on, if we make clear how impossible it is, with the least show of plausibility, to represent this letter as intended to teach the universal Church any matter of doctrine. It may be found in Baronius' Annals, A.D. 748, nn. 3—12.

The Pope begins by saying that he had heard from (St.) Burchard of Boniface's great trials in preaching the Gospel, and that he earnestly prays God to give him grace and salvation. "But there were inserted," he adds, "in those communications of thine various particulars, on which *thou didst desire the judgment and advice and consolation of the Holy See.*" Here at once that very feature is conspicuously present, which in Pius IX.'s letter just considered was so conspicuously absent: the Pope is giving practical directions to an individual prelate on particular cases. Firstly, he refers to certain false doctrines on the sacrament of Baptism, which Boniface had mentioned (n. 4, 5); and next to certain false priests who had deluded many (n. 6). He exhorts the saint to courage in all his trials, and entreats him to encourage the rest (n. 7). He then condemns the extraordinary tenet, maintained by Sampson, a Dutch priest, that a man may become a Christian without Baptism, by the laying on of episcopal hands (n. 8). He praises warmly a volume written by Boniface "on the truth of the Catholic faith" (n. 9). He declines to send a priest to France and Gaul representing the Holy See, being thoroughly satisfied with Boniface as its representative. He exhorts him, however, to hold provincial councils (n. 9). He refers again to Boniface's book (n. 10), and then proceeds to the case of Virgil.* This man had fostered enmity between Boniface and Duke

* Some writers have identified this unhappy man with St. Virgil, bishop of Saltzburg; but Pagi earnestly protests against this opinion, and Perrone thinks Pagi most certainly in the right. Apart from the historical inquiry, no one, we think, can read the Pope's letter, and believe that Virgil approached to sanctity ever so distantly.

Otho, and had reported himself to have been appointed by the Pope successor to a certain deceased bishop. The Pope assures Boniface that this report is totally false (n. 10). The same Virgil had been denounced by Boniface, in the letter to which this is an answer, as holding "a certain perverse doctrine against God and his soul,"—the doctrine, viz., "that there exists under the earth another world, and other men, and another sun and moon." The Pope enjoins Boniface to degrade Virgil from the priesthood and excommunicate him, if he be convicted of this opinion; and promises that he will himself look into the matter (n. 11). Indeed, on the whole case, not of Virgil only, but of another priest, Sidonius, he acknowledges the receipt of Boniface's communication, and says he has already written to them with severity. He exhorts Boniface, at the same time, to endure such men with gentleness and patience (n. 11). Lastly, he entreats the saint not to resign his bishopric, but to choose a worthy coadjutor (n. 12).

We will speak in the next Essay on Virgil's view of the antipodes. But we have risked wearying our readers by giving a full analysis of the letter, that the very miscellaneousness of its contents might be seen abundantly to evidence the truth of our conclusion. This is the question. Was Pope Zachary's letter "intended to inculcate some doctrine on the whole Church as theologically certain?" Or was it intended to convey personal guidance and exhortation to St. Boniface? The question may really be said to answer itself.

(5) We are inclined, however, to think, that the Pope does give a general test, whereby we may certainly

know that some letter, addressed to an individual bishop, is intended as an instruction to the whole Church ex cathedrâ. We speak here with diffidence, as we are not aware of any theologian who has treated the question; but we observe that in the recent Encyclical Pius IX. unites all the Apostolic Letters from which the Syllabus is compiled, under the common category of "*having been published* by him."* If the Pope writes to a bishop for his individual instruction, of course there is no secret in the matter, and the letter becomes universally known; yet its publication takes place by the mere force of circumstances. But if the Pope himself *commands* its publication and promulgation, by this very fact he seems to indicate, that the letter is not intended for the bishop alone, but as a public act affecting the whole Church. We shall see immediately that this view of the case receives great light, from a theological opinion held by many on the decrees of Pontificial Congregations; while reciprocally, if it be admitted, it will tend greatly to confirm that opinion.

It is now time to enter on a distinct but kindred inquiry. We have just seen that the Pope's letter to an individual bishop, is often, in fact, a doctrinal instruction addressed to the whole Church. May it not similarly happen, that what is in form the doctrinal decree of a congregation, is in fact a doctrinal decree promulgated by the Pope as Universal Teacher? We

---

* "Pluribus *in vulgus editis* Encyclicis, &c., errores damnavimus." We would submit whether the more natural translation of this would not be, "*by publishing* Encyclicals, &c., we condemned," &c. But it is immaterial to our argument.

strongly incline to think that under particular conditions this is the fact. Bouix quotes the following judgment of that very eminent and learned theologian Zaccaria (p. 472). The italics are our own:—

> Sometimes these decrees are issued expressly in the name of the Pope alone, the cardinals of the congregations being named therein only as examiners, who have given their judgments to his Holiness; as is seen in the decrees of Alexander VII., Innocent XI., and Alexander VIII. against certain propositions. At other times decrees *are published* in the names of the cardinals, but with the knowledge of the Pope, and *by his special order*. Some persons, it is true, will have it that in these two cases the Pope is to be considered not as head of the Church, but only as head and president of those congregations; and that, consequently, his infallibility does not inflow into such prohibitions: but it is also true, that the greater number have a different opinion on the subject, and maintain, *with much reason, that even in such cases the Pope acts as the infallible head of the Church.* . . . .
>
> There remain those prohibitions of the congregations which are issued with the assent of the Pope, *but not by his particular command.* These are *not* strictly [veramente] *infallible.*

Zaccaria mentions here three different kinds of doctrinal decree:—1. Those which issue directly from the Pope, after having consulted certain Congregations; 2. those which issue from a Congregation, but of which the Pope himself has commanded the publication; 3. those which issue from a Congregation with the Pope's assent, but which are not published by his particular command. The first kind does not here concern us: such doctrinal decrees can in no sense be called those "of a Pontifical Congregation;" and they are but particular instances of that far larger class, which we have been treating in earlier articles. That all decrees of this class are infallible, we have maintained in those articles to be beyond the possibility of question.*

Passing, then, to the two kinds of decree which do concern us, it is Zaccaria's doctrine, that decrees of a Pontifical Congregation, *which are published and promulgated by the Pope's express command*, are, in fact, his instructions ex cathedrâ and infallible. This doctrine, it seems to us, has received very great support, from Pius IX.'s language in speaking of Günther's condemnation. "Which decree" [of the Index], he says, "sanctioned by our authority, and *published by our command*, ought plainly to suffice, in order that the whole question be judged as *finally decided* [penitùs dirempta]; and that all who boast of the Catholic profession should clearly and distinctly understand, that complete obedience must be paid to it, and that the doctrine contained in Günther's books may not be considered sound [sinceram haberi non posse]." We do not see how the words "penitùs dirempta" can well imply anything less, than a final and absolute determination. It is so necessary, however, for the main purpose of our article, to make clear the distinction between the two kinds of decree, that at the risk of tediousness we will set down one or two rudimental truths, on which that distinction depends.

The Pope exercises two different functions, not to

* We do not understand how any one can possibly have supposed, that decrees addressed to the whole Church by the Pope, in his own name, are issued by him merely as head of a Congregation; because it is admitted by every Catholic, that if the Episcopate adhere to such decrees, they become the utterance of the Ecclesia Docens. We conclude, therefore, that Zaccaria, by some inadvertence, applied to the *two first* kinds what he only meant of *the second*.

speak of more—(1) that of the Church's Infallible Teacher; and (2) that of her Supreme Governor. The former he can in no sense delegate; but of the latter he may delegate a greater or less portion, as to him may seem good. Moreover, in either of these characters he may put forth a doctrinal decree; but with a somewhat different bearing. If he put it forth as Universal Teacher, he says, in effect, "I teach the whole Church such a doctrine;" and the doctrine is, of course, known thereby to be infallibly true. But if he put forth a doctrinal decree as Supreme Governor, he says, in effect, "I shall govern the Church on the principle that this doctrine is true." That the doctrine so recommended has an extremely strong claim on a Catholic's interior assent, is the very thesis which we are presently to urge: but, of course, it is not infallibly true; because no Papal dicta have that characteristic, unless the Pope utters them in his capacity as Universal Teacher.

We now come to the immediate question. Zaccaria's doctrine in itself is, at least, very plausible; viz., that if some doctrinal decree, drawn up by a Pontifical Congregation, is promulgated and published by the Pope's express order, it is infallibly true; because he is in fact (by that very order) directly addressing the Universal Church, as her Teacher.

But whether or no this can be maintained (which, at last, is of no very great practical moment), the latter part of Zaccaria's opinion is most indubitably true; viz., that no doctrinal decree of a Congregation is sanctioned by Papal infallibility, unless its promulgation is made expressly by Papal command. For such a decree in no sense comes to the Church immediately from the Pope; but from the Congregation, as his delegate. But in which capacity of his is the Congregation his delegate? Exclusively, as we have seen, in his capacity of Supreme Governor. Such a decree, therefore, is put forth by the Supreme Pontiff in this latter capacity; its doctrine has, no doubt, an extremely strong claim on a Catholic's interior assent, but it has not the promise of infallibility.

We are now to consider the interior assent due to these respective kinds of decree. And in regard to those which are infallible, of course the case is plain. Catholics are required to yield them a most unreserved interior assent, for that simple reason. The whole difficulty turns on those which are confessedly fallible. And here the reader should be reminded, that the question concerns doctrinal decrees expressly put forth, and nothing else whatever. As regards, *e.g.*, the Congregation of the Index, Catholics are not required to believe, as a matter of course, that any particular book really contains that particular tenet, which the Congregation may ascribe to it; though probably there never was a tribunal, whether you consider its constitution or its established method of procedure, in which there was better security for a true conclusion being reached.* But all this is apart from our present subject.

* The *Weekly Register*, of April 29, 1865, translates an admirable defence of the Index, published at Rome by Mgr. Nardi, in answer to the strictures of M. Rouland in the French Chamber. Bouix gives the following quotation from Zaccaria, on which we shall express some comment at the end of our article.

"And, generally speaking, when he (Arnauld) says that there may have been, or that there may be in future, unjust prohibitions of books at Rome (though not among those which emanate immediately from the Pope himself, ex cathedrâ, or from the Congregations

It is commonly asked, then, how interior assent can be claimed for a pronouncement confessedly fallible. Of course no one is required, or even permitted, to accept such pronouncement with that absolutely unreserved and unquestioning assent, which is due to infallibility. But take such an illustration as this. I have never studied medicine systematically; but I am fond of experimentalizing in a quiet way, and have come to an opinion that a certain remedy would be serviceable for a certain disease. I publish my opinion, with its grounds; and find it repudiated by every one, young or old, who has gone through a medical education. All combine to assure me that I am quite

---

[published] by his special order, and with his special approbation, for the entire Church), this author will not meet with much opposition from us; because into such judgments, if they are not supported by infallibility (although coming to us from highly respected persons), through the fault of the revisors, or through the mistaken impression of some judge, who is either unfair, or prejudiced, or timid, sometimes obreption or subreption may be introduced; and sometimes that "summum jus," which becomes "injuria." Prohibitions are not different in their nature from dispensations, which, generally speaking, may sometimes be unjust.

"But in the first place, those injustices which may sometimes corrupt a decree of prohibition, if regarding doctrine, could at most, I think, only exist *so far as there is attributed to an author some proposition which he really did not mean to advance, or which he certainly did not mean in the unsound sense which the censors attributed to him. But I do not believe this ever occurs with respect to doctrine, at least if it be theological or sacred; for I am convinced that it appertains to Providence not to permit that Rome, even apart from cases where the Pope speaks ex cathedrâ, should condemn as erroneous a doctrine which is not so.* Experience confirms my assertion: because it will be found that since the Congregations of Cardinals have been instituted, they have never, in any book, condemned a doctrine which did not deserve the censure."

mistaken, and that my reasoning is absurdly insufficient to establish my conclusion. No one alleges that God has endowed the medical profession with infallibility; and yet it would not be so much presumption as actual insanity, so soon as I am satisfied that they have really pondered what I have written, if I hesitated to abandon my own opinion in deference to theirs; and this, though I were wholly unacquainted with their reasoning, or could see no force in it. You cannot possibly allege, then, that the notion is in itself absurd, of interior assent being due to a fallible judgment. All that you can say is, that it is not legitimately claimed for that particular class of fallible judgments which we are now considering. We maintain that it *is* legitimately claimed for them; and on this alternative issue is now to be joined.

We must first, however, state clearly, what is the kind and degree of interior assent for which we contend. So much as this. Supposing some preconceived opinion of mine is condemned by a Pontifical Congregation: I should at once abandon all interior belief in the truth of that opinion; I should take for granted the correctness of the decree; and I should reconsider my grounds of conviction, with the full expectation of finding myself to have been quite in the wrong. More than this, we believe, is not expected; less than this, we are sure, is not reasonable. We will give three different reasons for our conclusion, either of which, we believe, would alone suffice.

(1) We have argued at length, in several recent numbers, for the doctrinal infallibility of an extremely large range of Papal declarations, which are not definitions of faith; and we have admitted throughout,

that our present argument entirely depends on the truth and certainty of this doctrine. Now such infallibility being assumed, even a slight acquaintance with the Papal documents in question will convince any man of one fact. Whoever heartily accepts them as infallible,—and has applied himself to studying them with that vigour and intentness which alone are reasonable on that hypothesis,—will have his mind imbued with a vast body of infallible truth, to which ordinary Catholics are comparatively strangers. It further follows from the same doctrine, that one only course is reasonable, in the case of any Catholic who (as the Munich Brief expresses it) "applies himself to the speculative sciences, that he may confer new benefits on the Church by his writings." He should study most carefully all those infallible pronouncements which bear directly or indirectly on his theme; submit his intellect most unreservedly to these, as being guaranteed to be true by God Himself; and conduct his whole argument with constant reference to their teaching. Putting aside the case of Galileo, which is "sui generis" and shall be separately considered, we entirely disbelieve that any person who has so acted has ever found himself, or ever will find himself, in conflict with a Congregational decree. The question therefore concerns the Catholic writer, who has *not* thus studied the relevant Pontifical declarations. Possibly he may not think these infallible: in that case, here is the whole root of the mischief; yet we admit that, while holding this unhappy error, he does not (so far as we see) add to his fault, by withholding assent from a mere Congregational decree. There remains then the supposition, that he admits the infallibility of this Papal teaching;

that he knows, or easily may know, the large extent of ground which it covers; and that he is conscious of having given it no careful study. Well: a body of men, who make it their business and profession to master it methodically, and who from position and association are singularly free from all sinister or non-Papal influence, decide that he has contravened it. It would surely be the extremity of unreason, if he did not yield to such a decision that full measure of assent which we have claimed for it.

(2) Such a decree further claims his assent on a totally different ground, as being the exponent of Roman tradition. "In which [Roman Church] always remains the infallible magisterium of the faith, and in which, therefore, *Apostolic Tradition has always been preserved*" (Encyclical "Nostis et nobiscum"). "In which [Roman Church] alone religion has been inviolably preserved, and from which all other Churches must borrow the tradition of faith" (Bull "Ineffabilis"). So authoritative is the endemic and pervasive tradition of the Roman Church. Now of that tradition, the various officials of the Pontifical Congregations, acting as they always do under the Pope's immediate supervision and direction, are the special depositaries and guardians. Where they speak, the voice of Rome is heard.*

---

* "The strength and authority of the judgments of Roman theologians are derived not from (so to speak) their personal learning and ability; but chiefly from the circumstance that those judgments may most justly be regarded, if not with absolute certainty, yet with great probability, as expressing the mind and sense of that Church, which is the mother and mistress of all Churches, and which (according to the condemnation of the proposition of Peter of Osma) cannot

(3) There is a third reason for our conclusion, more directly supernatural that either of the preceding; viz., God's special watchfulness over the Church's purity of doctrine. Take as an instance, all which Catholics of our day remember to have occurred on the Immaculate Conception. Pius IX. did not address the Church on this doctrine as Universal Teacher, before the memorable 8th of December, 1854: all the preliminary proceedings were enjoined by him in his character of Ruler. Yet as this series of commands had a special reference to purity of doctrine, what Catholic doubts that they were the very special concern of Divine Providence? What Catholic doubts that from the moment when Pius IX.'s active preparations for a definition commenced, a moral certainty arose — different in kind from any which previously existed—that the doctrine was really definable as of faith, and contained therefore in the Apostolic Deposit? In like manner the doctrinal decree of a Pontifical Congregation, sanctioned by the Supreme Pontiff, is itself, indeed, put forth by him in his capacity, not of the Church's Teacher, but of her Ruler. Yet its bearing on doctrinal purity is so close and indissoluble, that we may well share Zaccaria's confidence,* and believe that no real mistake will ever be permitted.

---

eit. 'Since the Roman See has been occupied by all S. Peter's successors, and by them alone, on this ground there accrues to this Church in comparison with others, *even without reference to the reigning Pontiff, the greatest brilliancy and the greatest authority;* inasmuch as it retains and represents that pure doctrine, which it has received from the continued series of Peter's successors.'—Delahogue." Murray, de Ecclesiâ, d. 17, n. 79.

* See note at p. 132.

These arguments, we really think, are so cogent, that no loyal Catholic would have felt one moment's difficulty in the matter, had it not been for Galileo's condemnation. To a consideration of this, then, we now proceed.

ESSAY VIII.

THE CASE OF GALILEO.

ON the matter before us, there are two altogether separate inquiries: firstly, the legitimacy and due effect of the condemning decrees at the time when they were put forth; and secondly, their legitimacy and due effect during the interval of time which subsequently elapsed, until their suspension by Benedict XIV. We will entirely conclude the former of these inquiries, before we enter at all on the latter. And we must make two preliminary explanations of our terminology. (1) It will be necessary, for purposes of convenience, to use the word "science," and its derivatives, in the sense which Englishmen so commonly give to it; as expressing physical and experimental science, to the exclusion of theological and metaphysical. (2) When we speak of a theory as "scientifically unlikely," we mean that the scientific grounds for its affirmation are weaker than those for its denial.

Now it is always desirable, for the sake of clearness, to keep the question of principle distinct from the question of fact. Before entering therefore on the history of Galileo's condemnation, we beg our readers' attention to those truths, theological and scientific, which will enable them (as we consider) more justly to appreciate it. We begin with the theological.

(1.) It is held by all thoroughly approved theologians, that Holy Scripture differs from all other books, in the fact that it is throughout the Word of God; that every proposition which it contains is infallibly true, in that sense in which God intended it. We are very far from denying that this doctrine, particularly in the present day, is surrounded with great difficulties, which require a controversialist's attentive consideration. But one matter must be treated at a time; and our present subject is not the inspiration of Scripture, but the doctrinal decrees of a Pontifical Congregation. The above-named doctrine then on Scripture will be assumed as true in every part of the following discussion.

(2.) The Holy Father is appointed by God guardian of the Apostolic Deposit; and it is his province, therefore, to warn Catholics against opinions and modes of thought which he may judge averse to doctrinal purity. But all the statements of Scripture, rightly understood, and the true doctrine, moreover, of Scriptural inspiration, are parts of the Apostolic Deposit. Hence, it is his province to warn Catholics against opinions or modes of thought which may tend to irreverence towards the Written Word.

(3.) Those controversialists, whether Catholic or Protestant, who censure the condemnation of Galileo, are in the habit of assuming, almost as a matter of course, that the Scripture texts, which were the ground of his condemnation, are manifestly irrelevant; that they merely purport to describe phenomena as such; and that in their simple and obvious sense, they would not be otherwise understood. So, among others, speaks Dr. Pusey, in his admirable volume on Daniel. We are amazed at this opinion. It may, indeed, be perhaps truly maintained in regard to Jos. x. 12-14, or Isaiah xxxviii. 8, which tell us of Josue's miracle and Achaz's sundial. Nay, it may perhaps be truly maintained as to most, or even all, of those texts which speak of the sun's motion. But consider the following: (Ps. ciii. 5), "Thou who didst found the earth *on its stable support* (super stabilitatem suam); *it shall not be moved for ever.*" (Ps. xcii. 1), "He hath fixed the earth *which shall not be moved.*" (Job xxxviii. 4-6), where God himself speaks: "Where wast thou," asks the Creator, "*when I laid the foundation of the earth? Upon what were its supports established?*" (super quo bases illius stabilitæ sunt?) Texts altogether similar are Ps. xvii. 16; lxxxi. 5; xcv. 10; cxxxv. 6; Prov. iii. 19; viii. 29. We entreat our readers to study successively these various texts.* It is most unfair to speak, as Dr. Pusey speaks, of "the mistakes of theologians," in the interpretation of these texts. Surely, had it not been

* We have cited them from a collection put together by the unhappy Passaglia, during the days of his orthodoxy, in an admirable note on Faure's edition of S. Augustine's "Enchiridion," p. 46. A still more copious assemblage of texts will be found in the article on "motion of the earth," which appeared in the "Penny Cyclopædia," and is attributed to Professor De Morgan. (Eccl. i. 4), "But the earth standeth for ever," viewed in its context, appears to us far less strong than those which we have chosen; though greater stress was perhaps laid on it by contemporary anti-Copernicans, than on any other. It should be observed, as will presently appear, that no ecclesiastical authorities cited any particular text; they speak generally of contrariety to Scripture.

for the Copernican theory, no one, who believes in the inspiration of Scripture, would have thought of doubting, that in them God expressly declares the earth's immobility. If any one hesitates at this statement on first reading them, he must be convinced, if he will put into words his own version of their meaning. Take *e.g.* the first: Ps. ciii. 5: "Thou who didst found the earth on its stable support; it shall not be moved for ever." This means, as we are now aware, "Thou who didst place the earth in its orbit; it shall not cease from steadily revolving therein:" but who will say that this is a sense in the slightest degree obvious?* And the same test may be applied with equal efficacy to every text we have named.

(4.) No inconvenience, however, arises, nor is there any irreverence towards God's Written Word, though this or that text be understood in a very unobvious sense, if that sense be affixed in deference to some definite, tangible, objective rule, the reasonableness of which is sufficiently established. It is, indeed, somewhat remarkable, that perhaps the strongest instance producible of this, is altogether independent of science and its discoveries. The Agnoëtæ were condemned as heretics, for holding that our Blessed Lord, in His

---

* We cannot give the Copernican interpretation a better advantage, than by quoting from Berthier's note on the verse. "This globe is placed on its own foundations; and *immovable in this sense*, that all its parts are maintained [in their mutual relations] notwithstanding the particular movements which take place on its surface and in its bosom. . . . Although our globe has two movements, the diurnal and annual, it subsists with all its parts without deflecting from the path which the Creator has assigned to it." Not an obvious paraphrase surely!

human nature, knew not "the day and hour" of divine judgment.* The Church, therefore, imperatively requires her children to understand Mark xiii. 32 in some very unobvious sense. But is there anything in this either unreasonable or irreverent? God surely has the right to interpret His own Word; for you would not deny this right to an ordinary mortal. Indeed, Catholics always maintain very truly against Protestants, that in several cases most serious error would be introduced, if Scripture were understood in some obvious sense, contrariwise to the Church's exposition. Now, the certainty of a scientific demonstration, though of a lower order than the certainty of faith, still is absolute; and the demonstration, therefore, of Copernicanism, should be reasonably taken as God's authoritative explanation of His own language.

(5.) But on the other hand, if a private individual may ascribe to any text of Scripture any unobvious sense he pleases—not in deference to some definite, tangible, objective rule, proved to be reasonable—but, according to his individual bias and caprice, the same result would practically follow, as from an actual denial of inspiration. We shall see immediately that in Galileo's time Copernicanism was "scientifically unlikely." If, on the strength of a theory scientifically unlikely, men are at liberty to contradict Scriptural texts as understood in that sense, which is both the only obvious one, and also the only one hitherto heard of in the Church,—what single text is safe? What is the difference of result, between openly denying the

* See Petavius de Incarnatione, l. xi. c. i. nn. 4, 15.

authority of Scripture in general, and explaining away every text one dislikes in particular? Such conduct is a very grave offence against faith; and it is the Holy Father's duty to put it down with a strong hand.

(6.) "The prevailing opinion in the Catholic Church as to what Scripture says on matters" appertaining to faith and morals, "cannot be false, for it embodies the teaching of the authorized exponent of Scripture. But it has never been denied, that the common opinion of what is asserted in Scripture on other points,—such as belong, *e.g.*, to the physical history of the universe—may be mistaken, and may be corrected and improved from time to time, by the progress of science, and the discoveries of history." *

(7.) The providence of God will, of course, secure that no Papal decision, claiming infallibility, contains false doctrine. Now, Paul V. undoubtedly united with the Congregation of the Index, in solemnly declaring that Copernicanism is contrary to Scripture. But we shall presently see it to be beyond the possibility of question, that this was issued as a doctrinal decree of the Congregation, and not as the Holy Father's infallible teaching.

(8.) Even before this decree, every Catholic was under the obligation of interiorly dissenting from Copernicanism. This is evident from what has been said. He was under the obligation of not disbelieving various texts of Scripture, in their one obvious sense, in the one sense hitherto universally received, when he had no warrant for such disbelief, except a theory which even

* *Dublin Review*, for October, 1863, p. 527. This passage was not written by the present author.

scientifically was unlikely. The Congregational decree added to the obligation in two ways. It emphatically and urgently impressed on his mind the obligation which otherwise existed; and, secondly, from that time forward, the recognition of such obligation no longer depended on his own personal judgment, but on the authority of the Holy See and of its most trusted advisers. Although he well knew that this judgment, in the shape in which it was given, was not strictly infallible, yet he also knew that, on a matter of Scriptural exposition, these authorities were immeasurably more likely to be right than a private individual.

(9.) But scientific truth cannot really be opposed to theological; and the Church could not rightly issue any command, which should prevent a full and searching scientific investigation of the Copernican hypothesis.

In addition to these theological principles, there are three scientific statements to which we beg the reader's attention.*

(1.) It is the business of a scientific man to pursue truth by scientific methods. One very chief scientific method is the invention of "hypotheses." No one, indeed, has a right to regard these hypotheses, while remaining merely such, as true or probable; yet they are most serviceable to science. It is found that some imagined property of nature, if it were but true, would account for a variety of phenomena, between which no

* It is more straightforward and satisfactory to state at once, that the present writer has no knowledge of physical science, which can warrant him in expressing any opinion of his own on such matters. He has taken, however, the best means in his power to insure scientific accuracy.

bond of connection has hitherto been discovered; or that some imagined physical law would be a far simpler explanation of certain multitudinous facts, than is any hitherto known. It would be monstrous to infer at once, merely from this, that the imagined property or law probably exists; yet the discovery is a most important service to science, as a clue to the ascertainment of fresh truths. When Copernicus found that his hypothesis afforded a far simpler explanation than any hitherto devised, for the motions of the heavenly bodies, he had every reason to rejoice in his invention, as being not improbably the herald of some eventful and critical era in astronomical investigation. But if, without any positive proof, he regarded his hypothesis as a probable truth, he was no less gravely censurable on scientific grounds than on theological.

(2.) We insist on the proposition, that simplicity is no proof of truth. A certain hypothesis explains various phenomena far more simply than they had hitherto been explained. This argument, under the most favourable circumstances, can never by possibility amount to a proof that the hypothesis is true. There is no imaginable link between premiss and conclusion, except by subsuming the further premiss, that God always acts by the most simple means; but this premiss not only has never been proved, but is pretty obviously false.*

* "We know well that nature in many of its operations works *by means of a complexity so extreme* as to be almost an insuperable obstacle to our investigations.

"The Sabean theory [*i.e.*, the theory of a non-omnipotent creator] is the only one by which the assertion that nature works by the simplest means *can be made consistent with known fact.* Even so, *it remains wholly unproved.*"—Mill on Hamilton, c. 24.

But in Copernicus', or even Galileo's time, this argument hardly furnished a presumption, much less did it establish a likelihood. The argument from simplicity may be thus stated at its greatest advantage. Let it be granted that some hypothesis, very far simpler than any hitherto devised on the same object matter, accounts for all the phenomena now known; let us further suppose that by assuming it freely and energetically during a series of years, men find that it would account for a constantly increasing number of phenomena, between which no connection has hitherto been observed; while, on the other hand, through all this time it has landed the inquirer in no conclusion antagonistic to known facts. We will not deny that from such circumstances there ensues a considerable scientific likelihood of its truth. But in Galileo's time there was no such reason whatever for counting the simplicity of Copernicanism as a reason for its truth. From the time, indeed, of Copernicus to that of Galileo himself, it did not account even for known phenomena: on the contrary, the fact that a stone when thrown up falls down on the spot from which it is thrown, *could be explained on the old system*, but could *not* be explained on the new.* Galileo invented a mechanical

* "The strength of the anti-Copernicans lay in this, *their unanswerable* argument of the throwing up a stone. Both parties believed that the stone of itself would not follow the motion of the earth; at least, such was the opinion *until the Galilean philosophy was fully received.*"—"Motion of the Earth," p. 458.

"In the sixteenth century the wit of man could not imagine how, if the earth moved, a stone thrown directly upwards would tumble down upon the spot it was thrown from. . . . The advocates of the earth's motion, before the time of Galileo, never even conceived" the doctrine which solved this particular difficulty; and let us grant for argument's sake (which is not entirely true, as we shall see), that from this time the theory (so to speak) started fair; that it comprehended all the known facts. It was possible, no doubt, that subsequent years would carry it through the brilliant and triumphant career, on which we can now look back: but there was then really no ground for even surmising this; there was no ground for even surmising, that it might not lead legitimately to one or to a thousand conclusions, which should be contradictory of undeniable phenomena. For centuries the rival theory had been found consistent with every new ascertained phenomenon. In Galileo's time Copernicanism was in this respect just entering on its trial.

It seems to us, indeed, that in Galileo's time the Copernican argument, founded on the simplicity of that theory, was much on a par with the anti-Copernican argument founded on the evidence of men's senses. Both arguments professedly appeal to the reason, while really they appeal merely to the imagination. "Can we fancy," asked the Copernicans, "that God has not acted on a scheme so impressive and so beautiful as ours?" "Can we fancy," reply their opponents, "that this earth is constantly in motion, which we feel to be the stablest of all things? that our senses are given to deceive us? that during great part of our lives we cling to the earth with our head downwards?" The reply to both arguments is the same. On such questions we have no means

law which explains this; "and, of course, never proved it."—De Morgan, "Notes on the Ante-Galilean Copernicans," p. 22.

whatever of arguing what God is likely to do: it is a matter for evidence, as to what He has in fact done.

(3.) So valueless in Galileo's time was the mere argument from simplicity. *Before* his time, indeed, it is not too much to say, that the Copernican theory was a mere guess, a mere conjecture. Listen to the chief arguments cited on both sides, before Galileo's discovery of Jupiter's satellites. We quote from De Morgan's "Motion of the Earth," using the letter C. for the Copernican argument, and the letter P. for the Ptolemaist opposed to them.

C. contended generally for the greater simplicity of their system and the incredibility of the enormous velocity which the sphere of the fixed stars must have if the Ptolemaic hypothesis were true: to which it was answered: P. That God doeth wonders without number. C. *That the earth would corrupt and putrefy without motion*, whereas the heavens are incorruptible. P. That wind would give sufficient motion. C. That *the most movable part of man is underneath*, since he walks with his feet; whence the most unworthy part of the universe, the earth, should be movable. P. [in addition to a good answer.] That if the earth moves, the head of a man moves farther than his feet. C. That rest is nobler than motion, and, therefore, ought to belong to the sun, the nobler body. P. That for the same reason the moon and all the planets ought to rest. C. *That the lamp of the world ought to be in the centre.* P. That a lamp is frequently hung up from a roof to enlighten the floor.—P. 47.

And such were the arguments, of which it has been gravely contended that they would justify Catholics, in disbelieving the obvious and traditional sense of God's Written Word! No doubt, Galileo considerably improved the scientific aspect of his cause; but what was it even in his time? It is thus summed up in an extremely able and fair paper in the *Rambler* (January, 1852). The writer quotes Delambre as his authority:

The Ptolemaic theory had sufficed for centuries to explain and to account for all the observed motions of the planets, as logically and as precisely as the Copernican theory does now; and it was during all this time found capable of taking in and preserving all the exact knowledge of the world. Such being the state of the case . . . a new system suddenly makes its appearance, and claims to supersede the old; and on what grounds? Because it accounted for phenomena in a more simple way than the old theory. But then the old theory *did* account for phenomena, however complex it might have been, and *simplicity is not always an infallible test of truth.* Again, it was in analogy with the newly-discovered system of Jupiter's satellites, and accounted for the moonlike phases of Venus which the telescope revealed. *And these three points constituted about the whole proof which Galileo could bring forward.* His other arguments, from the tides and magnetism of the earth, are all moonshine. The Newtonian theory of gravitation was then unknown; and the periods of the revolutions of the planets appeared quite as disconnected and random, as did the cycles and epicycles of the old theory. Newton first explained the one law on which the revolutions depended; before his time *there was nothing to make the Copernican system more plausible and reasonable than the Ptolemaic theory. The modern demonstrations of the annual motion of the earth,*—namely, the micrometrical observations on the discs of the bodies of the solar system, and especially the great discovery of the aberration of light, by which that motion is made evident to the senses,—*were then unknown:* and as to the diurnal motion, it was unproved till Richer's voyage to Cayenne, where he was obliged to shorten his pendulum. And it is only within the last few months that an experiment has been devised by which this motion may be exhibited to the senses, namely, by the apparent revolution of the plane of the vibration of a pendulum fixed over a horizontal table. *Before these demonstrations, there was no solid reason to induce men to disbelieve the evidence of their senses. The most decided Copernicans were reduced to mere probabilities,* and were obliged to confine themselves to preaching up the simplicity of the Copernican system, as compared with the absurd complexity of that of Ptolemy.* It is now generally taken for granted that the Copernican theory is self-evident. So far from that being the case, we may safely affirm that, *up to Galileo's* time, the balance of proof

---

* Delambre, Astron. Mod. Discours prél.

was in favour of the old system; that is, the old system was at that time *the* probable one, and Copernicus' theory the improbable one (pp. 15, 16).

But, fairly and temperately as this writer expresses himself, it would seem, nevertheless, that he states Galileo's scientific status at somewhat greater advantage than truth will warrant. M. Artaud, in his "History of the Sovereign Pontiffs" (Vol. V., pp. 316-321), draws attention to a paper contributed by M. Léon Desdouits, a Catholic savant, to the *Univers Catholique* of March, 1841. The *gravity of the air*, M. Desdouits reminds his reader, was first discovered by Torricelli after Galileo's death. The Florentine philosopher, therefore, from ignorance of this fundamental truth, was in an inextricable difficulty. To say that the earth is whirled through the terrestrial air, was plainly inconsistent with phenomena; while yet he could give no sufficient reason for supposing that the earth carries the air with it in its revolution. He was unable, therefore, to complete a theory of his own, which he could even reconcile with known facts; and since his opponents had no difficulty whatever in so reconciling theirs, it is not too much to say that his hypothesis, in its then incomplete state, was "scientifically unlikely"—*i.e.*, that there were stronger grounds for rejecting than for accepting it.*

* How *great* a difficulty in Galileo's way was the one here stated, is a question which we leave to the judgment of our scientific readers. A Protestant gentleman of great scientific eminence, whom we have consulted, considers that M. Desdouits has greatly overstated its magnitude. Apart from *gravitation* of the air, he says, there is its adhesion to solids, and a kind of friction against itself. All this would *tend* to produce Galileo's phenomenon, though, of course, inadequate, without adding gravitation, for the required result.

Lastly, we should not fail to point out that the particular argument on which he laid by far his greatest stress, is admitted by every one nowadays to have been absolutely valueless and irrelevant. We allude to that which he attempted to draw, from the flux and reflux of tides. His own confidence, therefore, in the scientific strength of his position, is no kind of argument for its real strength.

Let us now turn to the history of the case. Dr. Madden's recent work, "Galileo and the Inquisition," will be found a very valuable and interesting repertory of facts, though we regret to find ourselves not unfrequently differing from his judgment of them.* For ourselves, we shall consider them only so far as they bear on the theology of the matter.

Firstly, since so much has been said about the Church's unequal treatment of Copernicus and Galileo, let us speak of the former. We have seen that, if Copernicus merely published his theory as a most serviceable hypothesis, he deserved extremely great scientific praise and no kind of theological censure; but that, if he advocated it as a probable truth, he was both scientifically and theologically condemnable. Now, which of these was the case? Let us begin with Prof. De Morgan:—

When the work of Copernicus appeared in 1543 . . . it was neglected as a purely speculative trial of a strange and impossible hypothesis. In 1566 Ramus simply reproaches Copernicus with the

* If among any Protestants there still lingers the belief that Galileo was tortured or otherwise cruelly treated, we may refer him to Dr. Madden's work for the most complete refutation of such calumnies. He has done excellent service, both in this respect, and generally by his copious narration of facts.

gigantic character of his hypothesis, and says it would have been better to have taken one *nearer to the truth:* in a manner which implies that he thought *both were agreed as to what the truth really was.*— "Motion of the Earth," p. 454.

Indeed, it is perfectly certain, and admitted by all, that in his preface he declared himself to advocate it as a pure hypothesis, "which fulfilled the objects of submitting the orbits of the heavenly bodies more conveniently to calculation, but which need not necessarily be true, *nor even probable.*" (*Rambler*, p. 4.) It is said that this preface was not written by himself; but, as no one doubts that he sanctioned its insertion, such a fact is immaterial. It is alleged again, and, indeed, cannot be denied, that there are some few passages in his work, which in their more natural sense speak of his theory as probably true; but much stronger evidence must be adduced than we have seen, before we will admit that a grave ecclesiastic prefaced the great work of his life by a deliberate falsehood on the very fundamental thesis which he proposed to maintain.* A fact mentioned by Prof. De Morgan both confirms our scepticism, and generally illustrates our argument. He says that, with one single exception (Digges), all the admirers of Copernicus during the sixteenth century—*i.e.*, up to the time of Galileo—represent him as really holding what his preface declares. ("Ante-Galileans," p. 7, note.) Digges alone of them denied that Copernicus meant his asser-

* It is wonderful how ready sometimes are the votaries of physical science to invest their heroes with moral faultiness, for the sake of extolling their scientific perspicacity. A much stronger instance will presently appear in the instance of Galileo.

tions "only as mathematical principles feigned, not as philosophical truly averred." But we will not pursue this inquiry further. Since Copernicus in his preface explained himself as he did,—and since there was evidently nothing stated prominently in his work to force a different interpretation on the reader's mind,—no further defence is needed for the inactivity of ecclesiastical authorities.

Even as to Galileo, it is plain enough that he never openly expressed a decided belief in Copernicanism; * though there were very great suspicions of his intending to convey this opinion without expressing it. One strong corroboration of this suspicion was, that he applied himself to the task of harmonizing it with the Scriptures; which, of course, was an unmeaning procedure, if he treated it as a mere scientific hypothesis. And generally a movement seemed setting in, headed by Galileo, towards the advocacy of Copernicanism as really true.† The Church, as in duty bound, applied herself to check the growing mischief. Both the Congregations of which our present article speaks—that of the Inquisition and that of the Index—were called into action, but in somewhat different ways. The Inquisition took merely disciplinary measures; and the Index, indeed, took disciplinary measures, but it also issued a doctrinal decree. It would seem that the Holy Father commissioned the Inquisition to pursue the matter according to the ordinary course of that tribunal, while he chose the other Congregation as the

* A singular mistake has been made by the *Rambler* writer on this head, to which we shall presently refer.

† This fact, it will be presently seen, is stated by the Index in its disciplinary decree.

mouthpiece of his own doctrinal deliverance. It is only this latter declaration which strictly concerns us; but it will be more satisfactory if we take all the various facts in order.

Early, then, in 1616 the Inquisition, by the Pope's command, referred the matter to its theological qualifiers; *i.e.*, to certain theologians, whose business it was to give a theological opinion on such questions as the Congregation might refer to them. Their response is well known:—

> That the sun is in the centre of the world and immovable by local motion, is absurd, philosophically false, and formally heretical, because it is expressly contrary to the Holy Scripture.
>
> That the earth is not the centre of the world, nor immovable, but that it moves, and also with a diurnal motion, is also absurd, philosophically false, and, theologically considered, at least erroneous in faith.

This response received no special approval from the Holy Father, and we are at liberty, therefore, to form our own opinion on its merits. We would express, indeed, with great diffidence the criticism which we would suggest; and the theologians had probably many arguments before them, with which we are unacquainted. But we are unable to see why a severer censure should be expressed on the former than on the latter proposition. It seems to us, as we have already said, that the Copernican explanation of those texts which seem to affirm the earth's immobility, is far more unobvious than of those which seem to affirm the sun's motion. The question, however, is comparatively unimportant. That the theologians, under then circumstances, were perfectly right in condemning Copernicanism as theologically unsound, does not, to our mind, admit of question.

On February 25, 1616, a Congregation of the Holy Office, held in Paul V.'s presence, and acting therefore by his express sanction, founded on this response its practical resolve. In obedience to such resolve, on the following day Cardinal Bellarmine, having summoned Galileo to appear, addressed to him a mild admonition; and the acting commissary of the Holy Office, in the presence of notary and witnesses, commanded him altogether to avoid "the said false opinion;"* and announced to him that thenceforth he would not be allowed to defend or teach it in any manner, *i. e.*, even as an hypothesis, either by word or writing, nor to treat of it at all. To this Galileo promised obedience, and was at once dismissed.

Next comes the disciplinary decree of the Index, also issued with the Pope's sanction, and dated March 5, 1616. We copy this from the *Rambler* article:—

Since it has come to the knowledge of this holy Congregation, that the false Pythagorean doctrine, altogether opposed to the divine Scripture, of the mobility of the earth and immobility of the sun, as taught by Copernicus in his book *De Revolutionibus*, and by Diego à Stunica in his commentary on Job, is being promulgated and accepted by many, as may be seen by a printed letter of F. Foscarini, in which he attempts to prove that the said doctrine is *consonant to truth, and not opposed to Holy Scripture* :—therefore, lest this opinion insinuate itself farther, to the damage of Catholic truth, this Congregation has decreed that the said books of Copernicus and à Stunica

---

* "Ut omnino desisteres à dictâ falsâ opinione," says the decree of 1633, in recounting the past history of the case. The word "desisteres," and others similar to it, need not necessarily imply that Galileo had actually *professed* "the said false opinion;" and the facts presently mentioned in the text will show, that they were not intended to imply this allegation as being certainly true.

be suspended till they are corrected, and that the book of Foscarini, and all others teaching the same thing, be prohibited.

The gravamen of the charge, it will be seen, is that Copernicanism is advocated, not merely as a serviceable hypothesis, but as "consonant to truth, and not opposed to holy Scripture." Nor does the decree, we think, decide the personal question, whether Copernicus really intended to suggest the truth of his theory. It need only mean that his work contains certain passages which, taken in their objective sense, imply that assertion. "Cardinal Gaetani was" at once "employed" to make the necessary corrections in Copernicus's work; "and he carefully changed every dogmatic assertion" of the theory, "or any conclusion from it, into a merely hypothetical statement; after which the work was allowed."* Professor De Morgan adds ("Ante-Galileans," p. 6), that "the alterations *were very few in number:* and though confessedly disposed to cancel the whole of chapter eight, as treating of the truth of the motion of the earth, they [the Congregation] were nevertheless able to allow it to stand, because the author seemed to be speaking problematically; whence they only imposed a few verbal alterations."†

Lastly, comes the doctrinal decree of the Index, which would seem to have been issued simultaneously with its disciplinary decree. Of this, so far as we

---

* *Rambler*, p. 6.

† This decree makes evident, what is otherwise admitted by all; viz., that the prohibition imposed on Galileo against teaching the theory even as an hypothesis, was a personal penalty inflicted on him, and extended to none else.

know, the fullest extant account is to be found in Bellarmine's letter to Galileo. We copy this from Dr. Madden's translation (p. 121), with only one obvious alteration at the end.

We, Robert Bellarmin, having learned that the Signor Galileo-Galilei has been subjected to false imputations, and that he has been reproached with having made before us abjuration of his errors, and that by our order certain penances were imposed on him, declare conformably with truth that the said Galileo, neither before us nor before any other person whomsoever in Rome, nor in any other place that we are aware of, made any sort of retraction in relation to any of his opinions, or of his ideas; that no punishment or penance was inflicted on him; but that a communication was made to him of a declaration of his Holiness, our sovereign, *which declaration was promulgated by the Sacred Congregation of the Index*, from the tenor of which it results that "the doctrine attributed to Copernicus as to the pretended movement of the earth round the sun, and as to the place which the sun occupies in the centre of the world without moving from its rising to its setting, *is opposed to the Holy Scriptures, and consequently may not be defended nor held.*" In faith of which we have written and signed the present *propriâ manu*, the 26th of May, 1616, as here below.

ROBERT CARDINAL BELLARMIN. *

---

* From this letter the *Rambler* writer deduces (p. 5) his singular opinion—an opinion on which he bases much of his argument—that Galileo at this time was not required to withhold interior assent from Copernicanism, but only not to teach it. But firstly, such an interpretation of the letter is intrinsically self-contradictory: it represents Bellarmine as telling Galileo that the Pope has declared Copernicanism to be a tenet "which may *not* be held or defended," and at the same time *permitting* Galileo to "hold" it, though not to "defend" it. Then, secondly, on the preceding 28th of February—*i.e.*, a very few days before—Bellarmine, in obedience to the Holy Office, had enjoined Galileo to "depart" (recederes) from that false doctrine, to "desert" it (desereres), to "desist" (desisteres) from it. He certainly, therefore, could not on the present occasion have per-

Here, then, is a doctrinal decree of the Index, sanctioned by the Pope, that the new theory "is contrary to the Holy Scriptures, and may therefore neither be defended nor held." It will be seen, indeed, that this decree is a good deal more reserved, than the response of the Inquisition qualifiers; yet that its purport is very clear and unmistakable. We have already argued, that it was the one true doctrinal decision under then circumstances, and that interior assent was due to it from all Catholics. The only remaining question is (a most vital one, however) whether it were intended as an infallible pronouncement ex cathedrâ. The theological investigations with which we commenced this article, leave no possible doubt on the true answer. The whole question, as we have seen, turns on one single issue: whether the publication of this decree were or were not expressly and formally commanded by the Holy Father himself. Care is taken that its very form shall exclude the possibility of two opinions on the matter. The "declaration of his Holiness" was "promulgated"—*not* by his Holiness, but—"by the Sacred Congregation of the Index."

---

mitted him to hold it. Thirdly, and most importantly of all, Galileo adduced this letter of Bellarmine's for his defence before the Inquisition in 1633; whereas nothing can be more certain (as will be seen in the text) than that his defence at that period was a denial of his having ever accepted Copernicanism as a truth. It is quite evident that Galileo sought and obtained Bellarmine's certificate, for a reason just the opposite of that supposed in the *Rambler;* for the purpose of showing that he had never anticipated the Church's judgment, by advocating the *truth* of his scientific hypothesis. This also is M. Charles's understanding of Bellarmine's certificate, quoted by Dr. Madden (p. 121).

And it is truly remarkable that Zaccaria, who is so express in laying down that no declaration of this kind involves the Pope's infallibility, cannot be suspected of devising his doctrine for a solution of the Galileo difficulty; because (as we shall presently see) he was himself an anti-Copernican.

There is in fact but one objection on this head which can possibly be made. It may be asked whether contemporary Catholics, at all events, did not consider the judgment to be ex cathedrâ and infallible. And it happens fortunately (which might easily have been otherwise) that materials are extant enabling us most unanswerably to prove the reverse. If one theologian were more prominent than another in his opposition to Galileo, it was Bellarmine: yet his words are recorded by F. Grassi, also an opponent of Galileo's, to the following effect:—"When a demonstration shall be found to establish the earth's motion, it will be proper to interpret the Holy Scriptures otherwise than they have hitherto been, in those passages where mention is made of the movement of the heavens and the stability of the earth."* Again, a passage is extremely noteworthy which is cited by the *Rambler* writer (p. 9) from "Fromond of Louvain, a contemporary of Galileo himself, and a great opponent of the new theory":—

In a chapter of his *Anti-Aristarchus*, entitled "Whether the opinion of Copernicus is now to be esteemed heretical," after citing authorities on the affirmative side, he says: "But it seems that several learned Catholics in Italy, France, Germany, and Belgipm care very little for these authorities, grounding themselves on the persuasion that the authority of the Cardinals in defining matters of

* *Rambler*, p. 13.

faith is not the highest, nor co-extensive with that of the Pope. Moreover, they have a very plausible way of explaining the passages of Scripture which make against them. But these arguments do not make them sufficiently secure, because the Congregation acts with full Papal authority; and, as may be seen by the bull of erection in 1588, *the Congregation of the Index always submits its decisions to the Pope, by whom they are examined and ratified, and from whom they receive their authority.* According to this rule, the decree in question must have been examined and confirmed by the Pope, *by whom, therefore, the theory is denounced as false, repugnant to Scripture, and heretical.* Thus a severe man would judge. But," proceeds Fromond, "when I consider how circumspect and slow Popes usually are in defining matters of faith ex cathedrâ, *and that they always issue these decrees in their own, not in other persons' names,* I think that the censure must be somewhat softened, and the authority of the Congregation of the Index must be supposed not equal, but next to that of the Pope. So I would not yet dare to condemn the Copernicans of open heresy, *unless I were to see another more express decree emanate from the Head of the Church himself.* Nevertheless, the Copernican opinion is at least rash, and has one foot within the limits of heresy, *unless the Holy See determine otherwise.*"

Fromond, then, we see, draws the very distinction which we are now advocating on Zaccaria's authority: he decided that this declaration could not be ex cathedrâ, because Popes "always issue such decrees in their own, and not in other persons' names." Then Professor De Morgan quotes Riccioli (born in 1598), "one of the strongest theological opponents of the earth's motion," as follows ("Ante-Galileans," p. 24):—

Since *no definition of this matter has as yet issued from the Supreme Pontiff,* nor from any Council directed and approved by him, it is not yet of faith that the sun moves and the earth stands still, by force of the decree of the Congregation; but at most and alone by the force of the Sacred Scriptures, to those to whom it is morally evident that God has revealed it. Nevertheless Catholics are bound in prudence and obedience, at least so far as not to teach the contrary.

The Professor adds, that not only was Riccioli permitted by the censorship so to publish, but that "many others who went before him" had received the same permission. We regard, therefore, our point as proved, and pass on to the further history of these transactions.

It is often taken for granted by Galileo's admirers, that throughout he interiorly accepted Copernicanism as undoubtedly true. They represent him, therefore, in fact, as one of the most mendacious and cowardly poltroons, who ever appeared in public life; and we would fain, if possible, "deliver him from his friends." That he was greatly attached to the theory; earnestly desired the Church's permission to believe it; and would at once have heartily and delightedly believed it, could he have obtained this permission;—is clear enough: but to our mind it is by no means clear, that he was prepared deliberately to accept it in defiance of her authority. The certificate which he sought and obtained from Bellarmin, is one strong argument for our conclusion; and M. Chasles (Madden, p. 121) quotes the following from his private letter to a friend:—"None in the world," he writes, "can call in question my exemplary piety, and my implicit obedience to the commands of the Church." Lastly, nothing can be more express than his statement to the Holy Office in 1633.

Galileo being placed in the presence of the officers of the Inquisition, he was asked if he held or holds, and since when he held, the opinion of Copernicus. To that he replied: "Formerly, that is to say, before the decision come to by the Sacred Congregation of the Index, and before any injunction was communicated to me in relation to the subject, I remained indifferent and I held the two opinions of Ptolemy and Copernicus as disputable, because both one and the other could be true in point of fact—*in naturâ*. But since the decision above mentioned has been established by the prudence of superior authorities, all ambiguity has ceased in my mind; and I have held, as I now hold, for very certain and indubitably the opinion of Ptolemy—that is to say, the immobility of the earth and the mobility of the sun. (Madden, p. 102.)*

At all events, it is not less than monstrous to say, that on this latter occasion the Holy Office required him to retract an opinion which he had hitherto avowed; they did but require him to confirm by oath that statement—of his interior disbelief in Copernicanism, since its condemnation in 1616—on which he had stood throughout as on his one sole ground of defence.

As to this process of 1633, by far our simplest course will be to publish the decree with which it terminated, and also Galileo's abjuration. This decree is the most trustworthy authority for the facts of 1616; and our readers by perusing it, will be the better able to judge, whether we have fairly grappled with the facts of the whole case. We will draw special attention to a few passages by italics. The translation is founded on Dr. Madden's (pp. 107—113);

---

* Galileo's language before the decrees of 1616 seems to have been quite in accordance with this statement; for towards the end of 1615 he spontaneously applied to the Holy Office, to learn "what he should believe on the Copernican system." This is stated, on the authority of a letter from him to Renieri, in an early number of the *Dublin Review* (July 1838, p. 94). The article to which we refer expresses or implies more than one proposition, with which the present writer cannot concur; but it contains a large number of interesting and pertinent facts, and its perusal will throw (we think) much additional light on the general argument of our present article. Dr. Madden (p. 6) attributes its authorship to the late Rev. Mr. Cooper.

but we have made various changes, to bring it (as we think) into nearer accordance with the Latin, which he has also published (pp. 189—194).

SENTENCE OF THE INQUISITION.

Since you, Galileo, the son of the late Vincent Galileo, a Florentine, and seventy years of age, were denounced to this Holy Office, because you held as true the false doctrine maintained by many—namely, that the sun is in the centre of the world and immovable, and that the earth moves also with a diurnal motion; because you had certain disciples to whom you taught the same doctrine; because you kept up a correspondence on the same with several German mathematicians; because you published certain letters on the solar spots, in which you explained the same doctrine as true; also, because you replied to certain objections against you, taken from sacred Scripture, by glossing the same Scripture according to your own interpretation of it. Moreover, since a certain writing in the form of an epistle was shown, which appeared to have been written by you to a disciple of yours, and in it you had followed the hypothesis of Copernicus, containing certain propositions against the true sense and authority of the Sacred Scriptures.

This holy tribunal, being desirous, therefore, of obviating the inconveniences and prejudices which were arising and prevailing, to the injury of the Sacred Faith,—by the orders of our lord the Pope and of the most eminent cardinals of this supreme and universal Inquisition, by the qualifiers of theology two propositions were qualified, concerning the stability of the sun and the motion of the earth, as follows:—

1. That the sun is in the centre of the world, and immovable by local motion, is absurd, philosophically false, and formally heretical, because it is expressly contrary to the Holy Scripture.

2. That the earth is not the centre of the world nor immovable, but that it moves, and also with a diurnal motion, is also absurd, philosophically false, and, theologically considered, at least erroneous in faith.

But when it pleased us in the meantime to proceed mildly against you, it was decreed in the Holy Congregation held in the presence of the Holy Father, on the 25th of February, 1616, that Cardinal Bellarmin should enjoin you to keep aloof (*recederes*) altogether from the aforesaid false doctrine; and that, in the event of your refusing, the commissary of the Holy Office should order you to abandon the said doctrine, and that you should neither teach it to others, nor defend it, *nor treat of it;* and that, if you did not acquiesce in this command, you should be thrown into prison. And in execution of this decree, on the following day, in the above-mentioned place, in the presence of the Cardinal Bellarmin, you were mildly admonished by him, and commanded by the commissary of the Holy Office, before a notary and witnesses, that you should wholly avoid the said false opinion, and that in future you would not be permitted either to defend it nor in any way teach it, either orally or in your writings: and when you promised obedience, you were discharged. And, in order that so pernicious a doctrine should be taken wholly away, and no longer allowed to spread, to the great detriment of the Catholic Truth, a decree emanated *from the Sacred College of the Index* in which the books were prohibited which treat of doctrine of this kind; and that doctrine was declared false by *it*, and altogether contrary to the sacred and divine Scriptures.

And when finally this book appeared, published in Florence last year, the title of which showed that you were author of it, which title was "*Dialogo di Galileo-Galilei delle Due Massimi Sistemi del Mondo Tolemaico e Copernicano:*" and when, at the same time, the Sacred Congregation knew that, through the publication of that book, every day more and more the false opinion of the motion of the earth and the stability of the sun was disseminated; the said book was diligently examined: and in it was clearly found a transgression of the said precept, which had been intimated to you; and that you in the same book defended the said prohibited opinion, already condemned, and declared to you as having incurred condemnation. For as much as in the said book you tried to make it appear, by various circumlocutory phrases, that you leave that opinion as undecided by you and *expressly as probable;* which likewise is a most grave error,—*since that opinion can in no manner be probable which has already been declared and defined as contrary to Scripture.* Therefore, by our order, you were cited to this Holy Office, and on your examination on oath you have acknowledged the said book as written and printed by you. It has been also confessed by you that, about ten or twelve years ago, after the order before referred to was issued, you had begun to write the said book; also, that you asked for license to publish it—not, however, communicating to those from whom you gained that permission, *the prohibitory injunction that you should not hold, defend, or teach in any manner that doctrine.*

It has been likewise confessed by you, that in several parts of the said book the composition of the work was such, that a reader might think the arguments put forward on the false side to be so worded, as by their strength they might rather convince the intellect than be easily refuted—excusing yourself that you had fallen into an error, as you said, *quite foreign to your intentions*, from writing in the form of a dialogue, and on account of the natural tendency of every one to take pleasure in the subtleties of his own mind, and in showing his acuteness over that of others—in discovering ingenious arguments even for propositions that are false. And when it was intimated to you that the fitting time had come for your defence, you produced a certificate in the handwriting of Cardinal Bellarmin, addressed to you, as you state; procured, as you say, by you, *that it might defend you from the calumnies of your enemies, who had reported that you had been called on to make an abjuration, and had been punished by the Holy Office*—in which certificate it is said that you had not abjured, had not been punished; but only that a declaration made by the Holy Father, and promulgated by the Sacred Congregation of the Index, had been communicated to you, in which it was decreed that the doctrine of the motion of the earth and the stability of the sun was contrary to the Sacred Scriptures, and therefore might not be defended nor held.

Wherefore, as here there is no mention made of two particular articles of the said precept—that is to say, that "you should not teach" and "in any manner"—it is to be believed that, in the course of fourteen or sixteen years, those things passed out of your memory, and that, on account of the same forgetfulness, you were silent about that precept when you solicited a license for publishing the said work of yours. And this was not urged by you to excuse your error, but that it might be ascribed *rather to a vain-glorious ambition than to malice.* But this very certificate produced by you in your defence rather aggravates the charge against you: since in it it is declared that the said opinion is contrary to Scripture; and, nevertheless, you dared to treat of it, to defend it, and even to argue in favour of its probability. Neither does that permission [to publish] help you, so artfully and craftily won by you, since you did not make known the prohibition that had been imposed on you. But, as it appeared to us that you did not speak the entire truth with respect to your intention, we indicated that it was necessary to proceed to a rigorous examination of you, in which (without purging yourself from the other things which were confessed by you, which were pressed against you with respect to your intention) you answered catholically. Which things, therefore, having duly considered, and having examined into the merits of your cause, together with the above-mentioned confessions and excuses of yours, and whatever other matters should be rightly seen and considered, we come to the following definitive sentence against you :—

Invoking, therefore, the name of the most holy Lord Jesus Christ, and that of His most glorious Mother, always Virgin, Mary, by this, our definitive sentence, which sitting in council, and by the advice of the Reverend Masters of Theology, and of our doctors of laws, we publish in these written documents concerning this cause, and the causes in controversy between His Magnificence Carolus Sincerus, doctor of both laws, Fiscal Procurator of the Holy Office, on one part, and you, the accused Galileo-Galilei, of the other. . . . . we say, judge, and declare, that you, the above-named Galileo, on account of those things, proved in the documents of this process, and which have been confessed by you as above stated, *have rendered yourself to this Holy Office vehemently suspected of heresy*—that is, that you believed and held that doctrine which is false and *contrary to the sacred Scriptures*—videlicet, that the sun is the centre of the orbit of the world, and that it moves not from east to west, and that the earth moves and is not the centre of the world; and that *an opinion can be held and defended as probable, after it has been declared and defined as contrary to the sacred Scriptures.* And, consequently, that you have incurred all the censures and penalties, by the sacred, canons and other general constitutions and particular statutes promulgated against delinquents of this kind ; from which it is our pleasure that you should be absolved—provided first that, with a sincere heart and faith not feigned, before us you abjure, curse, and detest the above-mentioned errors and heresies, and every other heresy and error, contrary to the Catholic and Apostolic Roman Church, by that formula which is presented to you. But, lest this grave fault of yours, and pernicious error and transgression, should remain unpunished altogether, and for the time to come that by more caution you should keep clear of them, and should be an example to others that they should abstain from this sort of offences, we decree that by public edict the "Book of the Dialogues of

Galileo-Galilei" be prohibited—but you we condemn to the formal prison of the Holy Office during our pleasure. And, as a salutary penance, we prescribe that, for three years to come, you should recite once a week the Seven Penitential Psalms; reserving to ourselves the power of moderating, commuting, or taking away altogether or in part, the above-mentioned penalties and penances.

ABJURATION OF GALILEO.

I, Galileo-Galilei, son of the late Florentine, Vincent Galileo, seventy years of age, appearing personally on trial before this tribunal, and on my knees before you, most eminent and reverend Lord Cardinals, Inquisitors-General of the Universal Christian Republic into matters against heretical pravity, having before my eyes the Holy Gospels which I have in my hands, I swear that I always have believed, and now believe, and with the help of God I will always believe henceforward, all that which the Holy Catholic and Apostolic Roman Church holds, preaches, and teaches. But because by this Holy Office, subsequently to its being enjoined on me juridically that I should abandon that false opinion which holds that the sun is the centre and immovable—that I must not hold, defend, or teach in any manner, or by any writing whatsoever, the said forbidden doctrine, which is repugnant to the sacred Scriptures—I wrote, and caused to be printed, a book in which I treat of the same condemned doctrine, and adduce arguments with great efficacy in favour of it, not producing any solution of them—therefore I am judged vehemently suspected of heresy; that is to say, that I had held and believed that the sun was the centre of the world and immovable, and that the earth was not the centre and is moved. Therefore I,—desiring to remove from the minds of your Eminences and of all Christian Catholics this vehement suspicion against me, legitimately conceived,—with a sincere heart and faith not feigned, I abjure, curse, and abhor the above-named errors and heresies, and generally every other error and sect contrary to the above-mentioned Holy Church: and I swear never more in future to say or assert, orally or in writing, aught which can bring a similar suspicion on me; but, if I shall know any heretic or person suspected of heresy, I will denounce him to this Holy Office, or the inquisitors or ordinary of the place in which I may be. I swear, moreover, and promise to fulfil and observe entirely all penances adjoined me, or which may be imposed on me. But if it should happen that I act in opposition to my promises, protestations, and oaths (which God forbid), I subject myself to all penalties and punishments which, by the sacred canons and other general constitutions and particular provisions, are enacted and promulgated against delinquencies of this kind. So help me God and the Holy Gospels on which my hands are laid.

I, Galileo-Galilei above mentioned, have abjured, sworn, promised, and engaged as above, and in faith of these obligations I have signed the present autograph of my abjuration, and repeat the same word by word.*

As to this decree of 1633, the following circumstances are observable. (1) The Holy Office acted, of course, in virtue of a jurisdiction derived from the Pope; but there is no reference to his special approval, as there was in 1616. (2) Copernicanism is treated as a heresy, on the simple ground that every express statement of Scripture contains an immediate revelation from God; and that its contradictory is, therefore, heretical. (3) So far as the cardinals rest on any ecclesiastical pronouncement, it is not on the response of their own qualifiers in 1616, but on the declaration of the Index sanctioned by Paul V. (4) All their expressions, however, are quite inconsistent with the supposition, that they regarded this decree as the Pope's judgment ex cathedrâ. They ascribe that decree, in fact, to the Congregation of the Index, and not to the Pope. Yet (5) a certain considerable authority is claimed for it. "In no way," say the cardinals, "can an opinion be probable, after it has been declared and defined as contrary to the Scriptures."

We have been hitherto speaking on the effect of

* No one, we suppose, now credits the absurd romance about Galileo rising from his knees and saying, "E pur si muove."—(See Madden, p. 113.)

these decrees in regard to contemporary Catholics. We are now to speak of their legitimate bearing, during that interval which elapsed, between Galileo's death and their suspension by Benedict XIV. This seems to us, in fact, the only even apparent difficulty of the question; so transparently reasonable and legitimate was the course taken by ecclesiastical authority in the earlier period. On this new part of our subject we speak with much diffidence, as we are not aware of any Catholic who has hitherto treated it; but the general principles of theology seem to us fully sufficient to explain all which needs explaining.

We must commence by a certain definition of terms. The word "probable," in particular, must be excluded from our discussion; because, otherwise, incurable confusion would arise, between its theological sense on the one hand, and its sense so deeply rooted in popular English on the other hand. When an Englishman calls a proposition "probable," he always means, we think, that it is more probable than its contradictory. But this in theology would be "magis probabilis:" a proposition is "probabilis" which rests on solid grounds, even though its contradictory may rest on grounds still more solid. We may distinguish, then, four different stages of a scientific proposition. (1) It may be a "mere hypothesis," as Copernicanism was in the time of Copernicus. (2) It may be a "grounded hypothesis;" *i. e.*, it may have solid arguments in its favour, though as yet the opposite arguments are still more solid. Such was Copernicanism in the time of Galileo. (3) It may be a "likely hypothesis;" *i. e.*, the arguments in its favour may outweigh those on the opposite side, without being actually conclusive.

(4) It may be an established and demonstrated truth.

It is important to illustrate this, by the particular case before us. During the period which we are to discuss, the Copernican theory became scientifically more and more likely, till at length actual proof was obtained. Such proof was first given to the world in 1687; when Newton showed in the "Principia" that Hadley's observation of 1676, in regard to shortening the pendulum, proved the earth's diurnal motion. No proof of its orbital motion was published before 1727, when Bradley gave to the world his discovery on the aberration of light. A considerable period commonly elapses, before such proofs become generally known; and still more, before they become generally accepted: yet it is certainly a matter of surprise, that even so late as 1755, we find F. Faure calling on those who are "Copernicans and Newtonians from mere hearsay," "to bring forward at least, if they can, any demonstration drawn from astronomical observations, *which observations are not explained by either hypothesis.* For this fact," he adds,—*i. e.* that the observations are explainable on either hypothesis,—"is confessed by the mathematicians themselves, as many of them as are ingenuous, and of good faith."*

Further, a proposition may be *scientifically* likely, without being *actually* so. To take a most extreme case, it is imaginable in the abstract, that a proposition may be *scientifically* "likely," in an extremely high degree, and yet *actually* not even "grounded." How can this be? There may be some declaration of

* "Enchiridion," p. 47.

Scripture or the Church so peremptory and unmistakable, as to out-balance any amount of scientific likelihood; and to engender absolute certainty, that of such proposition there will never be discovered a scientific proof. We are far from meaning that such a case has ever existed, but it is imaginable in the abstract. When Galileo was required to deny that his theory was "probabilis," he was not required to deny that it was *scientifically* "grounded," but only that it was *actually* so. This is most plain: because the ecclesiastical objection was its contrariety to Scripture.

Now a Catholic of this intervening period had no concern with the Inquisitional decrees, either of 1616 or of 1633: these were purely personal to Galileo. Neither (still less) had he any concern with the theological response of the qualifiers in 1616; for this was not a congregational decree at all. The two which concerned him, were firstly the disciplinary, and secondly the doctrinal decree, issued by the Index in 1616. So far as the former affected him, it was only in his liberty of action; but so far as the latter, it affected also his liberty of thought. Now, there was a very important difference of circumstances between these respective decrees. The former, continuing as it did in force to the time of Benedict XIV., must be considered for all practical purposes to have been re-enacted by every successive intermediate Pontiff; but the latter was never repeated at all. And since it is the freedom of science for which our opponents are especially jealous, and which they especially represent as outraged by these decrees, we will begin by considering their legitimate effect on the action and thought of a scientific man, who should be duly obedient to the Church.

Firstly, then, as to the disciplinary degree. He was not permitted to express himself, as though Copernicanism were an *actually* "grounded" hypothesis. But he was permitted and encouraged to use the hypothesis most actively, as his clue to fresh scientific results; and to treat with most ample justice the scientific arguments for and against. He was fully permitted to maintain that Copernicanism was *scientifically* "likely" in the highest possible degree; but he was not (we imagine) at liberty to teach expressly, that it had received absolute and irrefragable scientific proof. We must maintain that in all this his liberty as a man of science was not restrained in any appreciable degree. To say that Copernicanism was *actually* "grounded," was to say that the declarations of Scripture, and the authority of the Congregation's doctrinal decree, were not sufficient to override his scientific arguments. But to enter on this question at all—to approach it ever so distantly—was to abandon his character of scientific man, and assume that of theologian. His only scientific restriction was, that he might not represent the theory as having received absolute scientific proof; and considering the above-mentioned circumstances, the hardship of this was not very great. He might earnestly maintain, that such and such a phenomenon was not explicable on the anti-Copernican hypothesis; but he was not allowed *in words* to draw the conclusion, that the Copernican hypothesis was scientifically demonstrated as true. He was not commanded or desired to keep back one single scientific argument, which told in its favour; he was not prohibited nor discouraged from exhibiting the force of that argument in the strongest possible light. If it be said that at all events no *advantage* was gained by the restrictions imposed on him, we shall reply to that objection in its proper place.

Next for the doctrinal decree. To simplify our statement, we will make the grotesque supposition, that one single man of science—an excellent Catholic—lived and pursued scientific studies through the whole period. He has the deepest deference both for the obvious and traditional sense of Scripture, and also for the doctrinal decree in question; and he enters therefore on his investigation with the fullest expectation,—nay, he considers it almost a matter of course, that Copernicanism will be sooner or later disproved. Still it is his duty to fix his eye carefully on every vestige of scientific argument, on one side no less than on the other; and he thus finds to his amazement, as years go on, that the scientific presumptions in its favour are rapidly accumulating, while no fresh difficulty is discovered. This circumstance compels him to ask himself, what is the theological weight in the opposite scale. He has well known from the first that the decree was no infallible pronouncement; and, again, he is either himself aware, or learns from theologians, that there is more than one text in Scripture (we gave a very strong instance in p. 143) which the Church has always understood in some more or less unobvious sense. He also learns from them the Catholic principle, which we have already stated (p. 144); viz., that the received and traditional sense of Scripture, on scientific or historical matters, is far less authoritative than on matters of faith and morals. Gradually, therefore, he comes more and more to think, that Copernicanism may very possibly turn out to be true. Yet, however great its scientific likelihood—while remaining mere likelihood,—we think he will shrink from forming a decided and confident opinion of its truth, until the Church gives him some sanction for such opinion. It is her office, not his, to determine the sense of Scripture. We fully admit, however, that, supposing him cognizant of an absolute scientific demonstration, there is no further room for doubt; since that cannot be theologically false which, by a rigorous scientific demonstration, is established as true. Here, however, we would draw a distinction. Those who are actually capable of appreciating this scientific demonstration, should of course interiorly accept the truth of Copernicanism. But the mass of men are quite differently circumstanced: they must still choose between one authority and another; and we think they will act more perfectly, if they abstain from any absolute acceptance of the new theory, till they have obtained some guidance from the Church.

This will be our best place for inserting the well-known protestation of Newton's Catholic editors, in 1741. It is prefixed to the third book of the "Principia":—

Newton in this book assumes the hypothesis of the motion of the earth; and the author's proposition could not be explained except upon the same hypothesis. Hence we have been compelled to act a part (alienam coacti sumus gerere personam); but we declare that we obey the decrees that have been made by the Supreme Pontiffs against the motion of the earth.

The obvious meaning of which protestation we take to be this: "Had we been writing a scientific treatise of our own, we should have adduced indeed all the scientific arguments we know in favour of Copernicanism; but we should have deferred to the disciplinary decree now in force, by abstaining from all language which might imply its actual truth. Newton, however, of course, expresses himself quite differently; and since we are but his commentators, it was impossible for us to avoid expressing ourselves as he does: but we hereby protest that we have had no intention of publicly uttering any opinion whatever, on the actual truth of Newton's theory."

Just as scientific men will be always disposed to give scientific reasons a very undue preference over theological, so will theologians be ever disposed to give theological reasons a somewhat undue preference over scientific. Both classes are naturally far more struck by that particular kind of argument, with which their habits render them familiar. We cannot be surprised, then, at Passaglia's statement, that when Faure wrote his work (in 1755), the theological schools were commonly averse to the Copernican hypothesis. It will be more satisfactory, however, if we consider in the case of theologians, what we have already considered in the case of astronomers; viz., the legitimate effect on them of the two decrees.

As to the doctrinal decree, its legitimate effect on both classes of men seems to us much the same. But the disciplinary decree limited the free speech of theologians immeasurably more than of astronomers. The latter, as we have seen, were free to express the scientific likelihood of Copernicanism as strongly as ever they pleased; but however much disposed a theologian might have been to think, at some given time, that the scientific arguments for its truth reasonably outweighed the theological arguments for its falsehood, he was prevented from publicly stating that opinion. Of course he might freely express it in private conversation with other theologians, or might communicate it to the Holy Father; and, indeed, it must have been some such pressure of theological opinion, which led Benedict XIV. to suspend the decree.

It will be asked, what was its advantage at last? Of course we are here to assume the Church's teaching: viz., that books, theologically unsound, should be kept from those Catholics who are not specially qualified to read them without injury; and that liberty of the press "can never sufficiently be execrated and detested."* Now, in Galileo's time, all books which advocated the truth of Copernicanism, were theologically unsound. And a most important service was done, by preserving the Catholic flock free from the plague; free from a most false, proud, irreverent, and dangerous principle of Scriptural interpretation.

But should the decree have continued so long in force? On such matters of mere prudence, no one maintains that the Church is infallible; and looking back from our present vantage-ground, we are inclined to submit, that the supreme authorities would have acted wisely in suspending it some forty or fifty years sooner than they did. But this is a matter of detail, not of principle. Our general notion is this. The following, as we have already mentioned, may be called

* Encyclical "Mirari vos."

the two opposite poles of relevant doctrine. On the one hand there is neither inconvenience nor irreverence, in ascribing to the purely physical statements of Scripture a new and unobvious sense, if that sense be affixed in deference to an absolute and irrefragable scientific demonstration; yet, on the other hand, to do this on the strength of a theory which scientifically is not even likely, is unsound, censurable, and most dangerous. If it be asked, as a question of doctrine, at what precise point the line is to be drawn—what is the *degree* of scientific likelihood which would legitimize a change of Scripture interpretation—we frankly reply that we know not the definite answer; but if it be asked, as a matter of discipline, what practical course was desirable under circumstances, it was plainly (we think) the wise course to continue the disciplinary decree as long as possible. Who were injured by its continuance? Not scientific men; for they had full liberty to bring forward every scientific argument they could wish: not theologians; for the great majority of them disbelieved Copernicanism altogether: not the mass of uncultivated Catholics; for it would be absurd to say that they had any power of judging rightly on the question. Further, without censuring any who acted differently, we would strongly maintain that those took the more perfect course, who withheld full interior assent from a theory apparently so unscriptural, until they were cognizant of some rigorous scientific proof. On the other hand, the danger of removing the prohibition was most serious. For what would the Church declare by such removal? That an important series of Scripture texts might be lawfully understood in a sense most opposite to their obvious and their traditional acceptations; in a sense which had hitherto been regarded as unsound. Now the multitude of men, whether Catholic or Protestant, are very unfitted for drawing nice and accurate distinctions: they could not be expected to discriminate between one class of texts and another; or readily to understand how change of circumstances could justify the Church, in revolutionizing her practical guidance on a somewhat important question. So violent a shock to received ideas and to traditional religion, was not unlikely to issue in consequences so serious that authorities were bound to delay their act until the latest possible moment. When a complete scientific proof of the new theory was propounded, and was accepted by scientific men,—then, and not till then, came the appropriate time for action. As a matter of fact, the suspension was delayed somewhat longer: "Pope Benedict XIV. suspended the decrees; and in 1818 Pope Pius VII. repealed them in full consistory."*

"But can it be denied that the Church's acts of 1616 seriously retarded the triumph of Copernicanism?" Let us, for argument's sake, admit it, and what follows? The acts in question were put forth, for the purpose of repressing a method of interpreting Scripture, which was most unsound and uspeakably dangerous: viz., the departing from its obvious and its traditional sense, on the strength of a scientifically

* *Rambler*, p. 23. In 1744 Galileo's famous dialogue was published entire at Padua, "with the usual approbations."—(Artaud, p. 307.)

unlikely theory. We must be excused for thinking, that true principles of Scriptural interpretation are immeasurably a more precious possession, even than scientific truth.

But it may well be doubted, whether the Church did retard the progress of scientific truth. What retarded it was the circumstance, that God has thought fit to express many texts of Scripture, in words which have every appearance of denying the earth's motion. But it is God who did this, not the Church; and, moreover, since He thought fit so to act as to retard the progress of scientific truth, it would be little to her discredit, even if it were true that she had followed His example.

At least, however, "it will not be denied that the history before us is a significant warning against Ultramontanism. It was precisely those who most earnestly laboured to be in harmony with the Church's mind and the spirit of Rome, who were slowest in accepting the newly-discovered truth." We should be very sorry if the latter fact could with truth be denied. God has put forth certain utterances, which have every appearance of declaring the earth's immobility. The course of all others most consistent both with reverence and with reason, was to abstain from interpreting these passages in an unobvious sense, until some irrefragable scientific proof of Copernicanism were given. This was evidently the animating principle of what the Church did; and this, therefore, was the lesson learned, by those who most assiduously studied her spirit.

Lastly, it has been objected against this whole series of ecclesiastical events—we are quoting the very words of an eminent anti-Catholic philosopher—that "it necessarily tells much against the claims of those who should be at least among the wisest of men, if they used their authority against what the result proved to be the real direction of truth and progress." Certainly, it would tell against those claims, if the Church had ever professed to enjoy any special privilege of discerning "truth" in the purely physical and material order. But the reverse is notorious; she claims authority, as all the world knows, over those things alone which appertain, directly or indirectly, to the region of faith and morals. We are far from meaning by this, that her sphere is narrow or confined; on the contrary, those things which bear indirectly on faith and morals are enormously numerous. We are still further from sympathizing with those unsound Catholics, who will question this or that ecclesiastical decision, on the ground of its dealing with matters external to the spiritual order; for it is a first principle of Catholicism, that the Church, by the very fact of pronouncing a decision, pronounces also that the decision is within her province. Still, what the Church has testified of herself in every age, would lead us as little to expect from her any superhuman sagacity on the earth's motion, as on the electrio telegraph, or on the properties of gas.

But, at the risk of being charged with paradox, we must soberly maintain, that in no part of her history has she more conspicuouly displayed her divine gifts, or exhibited in her conduct móre unsmistakable marks of an overruling Providence, than in her whole treatment of the theological questions which concerned Galileo. The great principle on which she then proceeded, she maintains no less firmly in the nineteenth century than she did in the sixteenth; viz., that it is unsound and censurable to contradict the obvious and traditional sense of Scripture, on the strength of a theory scientifically unlikely. That which has changed in the interval, is no theological principle, but only a scientific fact; the fact, namely, that Copernicanism is now not scientifically unlikely, but, on the contrary, a scientifically established truth. Then, amidst what was pitfalls she was walking, throughout the whole of Galileo's career! a single false step and all was lost.* We will mention two circumstances in particular. Consider how anti-Catholic a position the Copernican party was assuming; consider, on the other hand, how confident were the Pope and ecclesiastical authorities that its tenet was condemned by Scripture. How truly remarkable, that no adverse decision was put forth, for which any one could even claim infallibility! that the decree issued was Congregational and not Pontifical! Then, again, earnestly desirous as they were to crush the "anti-Scriptural" error, and firmly as they were persuaded that it was philosophically baseless no less than theologically unsound, surely the one natural thing for them to do, was to prohibit Catholics from publishing any scientific argument in its behalf. Yet, in the very height of their anti-Copernican zeal, they were withholden from this indefensible measure; and they allowed consistently throughout the fullest and freest

* Humanly speaking, of course. We are arguing that God infallibly preserved her from any such false step.

scientific discussion of the theory. Who can fail to see in all this the finger of God?

Some lynx-eyed critic may, indeed, think to catch them tripping; and may point out that they exceeded their province, by condemning Copernicanism philosophically as well as theologically. But this very criticism draws attention to another argument in our favour. For who made this mistake? Firstly, the theological qualifiers of the Inquisition; learned and accomplished men no doubt, but of whom no one has ever alleged that they were instructors of the Church. Secondly, to some extent, perhaps, the two Congregations, in the *preamble* to their *disciplinary* decrees; and here again it is notorious that the preamble, even of a doctrinal decree, is never understood as authoritatively teaching doctrine. What, then, was the doctrinal guide of contemporary Catholics, alone recognised as such? Undoubtedly and notoriously that doctrinal decree, which the Congregation of the Index promulgated under Paul V.'s sanction. But this decree totally avoids the dangerous and untheological confusion; and condemns the new theory on no other ground, than that of its contrariety to Scripture.

We are now then in a position to draw out somewhat more accurately the doctrine which we sketched in a former article, on those doctrinal dicta of Popes which are not definitions of faith. We would premise, as we stated in that article (p. 39 of this volume), that we use the word "doctrine" and its derivatives to include, not merely that which is "directly" doctrinal—*i. e.*, which is actually part of the Apostolic Deposit—but that also which is "indirectly" doctrinal; *i. e.*, which is intimately bound up and connected with the former. A very large number of philosophical truths, of politico-religious truths, of dogmatical facts, are all included under the head of "doctrine." We next entreat our reader to peruse the remarks which he will find in pp. 50 and 51. And we will thus complete what we have there stated; recapitulating, for that purpose, much which has been urged in the article now drawing to an end.

Three different species may be considered of those Papal doctrinal dicta, which are not definitions of faith. We are referring of course, not to those doctrinal dicta, which a Pope may put forth as a private doctor writing a theological essay; but to dicta uttered by him in his official capacity. The first species of these dicta includes all those which are pronounced ex cathedrâ, and are therefore infallible. This species is subdivided into two different classes. The former class consists of those which are expressed directly by the Pope, in his capacity of Universal Teacher. Most of these are in the form of Allocutions, Encyclicals, and the like; and bear their own evidence of being intended for the whole Church. Some, however, are in form addressed to individual pastors or nations in the Church; and it may not be always absolutely certain, which of these are ex cathedrâ. Most commonly, however, their contents will make this sufficiently clear: moreover, it is not improbable that the Pope supplies some test of this distinction; and that all are ex cathedrâ, *of which he himself commands the publication*. These, then, make up the former class, included in the first species; while the latter class comprises those doctrinal decrees of Papal congregations, which are promulgated by the Pope's express command. This whole species then—containing the two above-named classes—is infallible by divine promise; and every Catholic, therefore, is bound to accept the whole of them, with the most unreserved and absolute interior assent.

The second species consists of "*obiter dicta;*" of Scriptural, theological, philosophical *arguments; preambles* to a decree; and the like. "Many statements, even doctrinal statements, may be introduced, not as authoritative determinations, but in the way of argument and illustration." * In these, the Holy Father is not professing to give any doctrinal guidance at all; and there is no difficulty whatever, therefore, in admitting, that they may be more or less mistaken.

The third species holds an intermediate place between the two first. The dicta which it includes are not expressed ex cathedrâ, and therefore are not infallible; yet, on the other hand, they are intended as direct inculcations of Catholic and obligatory doctrine. This species, like the first, is subdivided into two classes. The former class includes doctrinal statements put forth by the Pope himself, but not as Universal Teacher; put forth in pastoral addresses to this or that individual or church, with the view of preserving purity of faith or expelling doctrinal error. In the latter class, we place those doctrinal decrees of Pontifical Congregations, which are sanctioned by the Pope, but not promulgated by his express command.

---

* See this question admirably handled in Dr. Murray's "De Ecclesiâ," c. 17, n. 262—270.

It will be clear to every one, we think, that both these classes stand in the same category; but as more is said by theologians of the latter class than of the former, we will consider it first.

Of these congregational decrees, then, Zaccaria says, as we have already seen (see note to p. 132) that "it appertains to Providence not to permit that Rome, even apart from cases where the Pope speaks ex cathedrâ, should condemn as erroneous a doctrine which is not so." Bouix understands him to mean by this, that they are in some sense infallible: but, as we have said, the word "infallible" surely implies, not the mere fact of inerrancy, but the divine promise of inerrability; and this Zaccaria's words do not claim for these decrees. At the same time, even in his own sense, no Catholic of the present day can precisely accept his remarks, because of this very case of Galileo. Zaccaria himself was no doubt a hearty anti-Copernican, and had, therefore, no difficulty in the matter; but almost all Catholics at this day are Copernicans as a matter of course. Yet, with a very little change, we think that his remark may stand, and that it conveys a very important truth. We would say this, then, in regard to the doctrinal decrees of a Pontifical Congregation: there is no promise of their inerrability; yet we may humbly hope and expect, that God will at no period permit them to err in the doctrinal guidance which they give, regard being had to the circumstances of the time. Most certainly we must maintain that the decree against Galileo is no exception to this statement: on the contrary, it afforded true doctrinal guidance to contemporary Catholics; and was, in fact, the one legitimate application of Catholic principle, to the circumstances with which it dealt.

Zaccaria's reason for his statement, as we have seen, is his persuasion of God's special watchfulness over the doctrinal purity of Rome. We have already (pp. 136-7) drawn out two arguments, which were possibly both of them in his mind, when he expressed his judgment. And it is plain that the same arguments hold, not merely of these Congregational decrees, but (with still greater force) of those doctrinal instructions, which the Pope authoritatively addresses to a single church or to an individual Catholic. Our general doctrine, therefore, is this. By fully submitting ourselves to the Pope's doctrinal guidance, even in cases where that guidance is not strictly ex cathedrâ, there is every reason to expect that we shall assuredly be led aright; that we shall be led to that doctrine which, under the circumstances contemplated by him, is alone true.

Let us apply this doctrine to another instance, which has come before us in this article; viz., Pope Zachary's condemnation of Virgil. You may sometimes hear Protestants speak of the latter as deserving high scientific praise, for his belief in Antipodean men. This shows the blinding force of prejudice. Suppose he did believe the existence of such men, it could only have been by the merest guess; he had access to no scientific proof of it whatever. Surely it is the excellence of a scientific man, as such, that he proportions the strength of his conviction to the strength of his reasons, and not that he jumps to a conclusion by guesswork. Yet the same writers will moralize over the "darkness," the "narrow-mindedness," of S. Boniface or Pope Zachary. Certainly these holy persons did not know of Antipodean men; but neither did Socrates, Plato, or Aristotle: were the latter therefore narrow-minded and in the dark? Protestants, however, are commonly far more indulgent to a godless Pagan than to a Catholic Saint.

Now to the question. Virgil held "that under the earth is another world, and other men, and *another sun and moon.*" Why did the Pope and S. Bonifice consider that this implies some grievous error? Perrone * gives the obvious reason; that, since no one at that time dreamed of any possible communication between two opposite surfaces of the earth, Virgil quite certainly held that there were men on this earth not descended from Adam. Under those circumstances, therefore,—in the then state of physical knowledge,—any doctrine whatever of Antipodean men implied theological unsoundness. And since, in the earlier part of our article, we showed that there was no pretence for representing Pope Zachary's letter as an instruction ex cathedrâ, in strict necessity no more need be said on the matter.

We fully admit, of course, or rather maintain, that Divine Providence will never permit the Pope to issue any declaration as Universal Teacher, condemning a scientific tenet which may afterwards turn out to be true. But really, so far as its condemnation of Virgil goes, there is no reason why Zachary's letter might not have been ex cathedrâ. "That under the earth is another sun and moon"! A modern man of science would be as much aghast at such a notion (though on very different grounds) as was S. Boniface himself.†

---

* De Deo Creatore, n. 289.

† The *Rambler* says (p. 20), we know not on what grounds, that

Our practical conclusion is this. For doctrinal guidance—using that word in its largest legitimate sense—let us ever fix our eyes steadfastly on the Holy See; let us ever listen eagerly and with docility to the voice of Rome. Peter lives and teaches in his successors. He teaches, not only when they lift up their voice to address the Universal Church, but when they impart Apostolic Truth to individuals who seek it at their hands. Nay he teaches by their very acts of government; by the doctrinal principles on which they rule the Church. "As Rome acts by her strong words, so also she speaks by her strong acts."*

The particular instance of Galileo has been (especially of late) confidently, and with an air of triumph, held up before public attention, as a palmary and conclusive refutation of these "exaggerated pretensions." We have not chosen then our own battle-ground; we have advanced to the attack of that fortress, which the enemy values as his chief stronghold. It must be for others to decide, whether our attack has on the whole been unsuccessful.

---

the Pope misunderstood Virgil's meaning. At all events, the fact would be irrelevant; for that tenet which he condemned—whether Virgil's or no—is beyond question extravagantly false.

* Abbé Morel.

ESSAY IX.*

REPLY TO TWO OBJECTIONS.

THE article on Galileo in our last number was intended to close a short series, on the deference due to those Papal decisions of doctrine, which are not actual definitions of faith; and it dealt particularly with a case which, far more than any other, has been alleged as proving that such decisions are not infallible. On both these questions a few last words are necessary.

Our general thesis was, as our readers may remember, that the Holy Father is not infallible only when he condemns some tenet as heretical, but equally so when he brands it ex cathedrâ (as he often does) with a lower theological censure. Consequently, that any doctrine which he teaches in Allocutions, Encyclicals, and other pronouncements put forth by him as Universal Teacher, is none the less infallibly true, though its contradictory be not condemned as actually heretical. To this statement an objection has been made, which we had not thought of treating, but on which stress is laid by some sincere searchers for truth. We will now, therefore, supply the omission.

* Jan., 1866, "Appendix to the October article on Galileo."

Here is the objection: Ultramontane controversialists constantly assert that no Papal declaration is ex cathedrâ, unless it expresses or implies an anathema on the tenet which it condemns. Without crowding our pages with a series of extracts, F. Perrone may well stand as representing a class. These are his words:—

"By the name of a definition put forth ex cathedrâ, is signified a decree of the Roman Pontiff, whereby he proposes to the universal Church something *to be believed* [*as*] *of faith*, or to be rejected as *contrary to the faith*, under penalty of censure or anathema" (De Locis, n. 726).

Where the word "censure" seems used synonymously with that of "anathema."* The strongest Ultramontanes, then, it is argued, do not consider the Pope to speak as Universal Teacher, when he pronounces a lower censure than that of heresy. We shall maintain, in reply, (1) that all these passages are capable of an interpretation totally different from that which the objector supposes; and (2) that this different interpretation is most unquestionably the true one. We do not deny, of course, that a few theologians have *really* denied the Church's infallibility in these minor censures: on the contrary (see p. 111), we have quoted Dr. Murray's statement, that

* Many approved theologians use language which appears even more unmistakable. Take Antoine, whom we happen to be consulting on another point: "The supreme Pontiff is said to speak ex cathedrâ when, as Supreme and Universal Pastor, he defines something to be believed and held by all the faithful with certain faith, . . . in such sense *that he wills all who think otherwise to be separated from the Church's communion*" (De Fide, c. 5, a. 6).

he found three who did so; though not one of the three could rank as an "approved" writer. But as to the eminent authorities on whom our present objector lays stress, we are most confident that they would have been unspeakably surprised, had his interpretation of their meaning been ever presented to them as authentic. We believe the thing to have happened as follows:—

There are two questions, totally distinct from each other, and requiring an examination altogether distinct:—the "subject" and the "object" of infallibility. When I am considering the former, I am considering who *possesses* infallibility; whether, *e. g.*, the Pope alone, or not without episcopal concurrence: but when I am considering the latter, I am considering *over what objects* infallibility extends; whether, *e. g.*, it is confined to definitions of faith, or reaches much further. The former question is now of much less practical moment than once it was, because the Catholic Episcopate invariably assents to all Papal judgments; whereas the latter question is now, it may almost be said, more urgently important than any other whatever.

But in the great controversy between Ultramontanes and Gallicans, which raged so actively two centuries ago, the fact was notoriously just the reverse. To this day, a "Gallican" means, not one who limits the "object" of infallibility, but one who maintains that the Pope is not infallible when speaking ex cathedrâ. We are perfectly confident that on both sides it was an admitted principle, that the same authority which is infallible in condemning tenets as heretical, is no less infallible in pronouncing on them some inferior censure.* But this particular matter was hardly alluded to; the question which agitated men's minds being quite different. "Can the Pope infallibly condemn heresy?" was the issue, "or is his condemnation liable to error, unless the Episcopate assent?" The Ultramontanes admitted, of course, that the Pope was not infallible, unless he spoke ex cathedrâ. "But how do you know whether he is speaking ex cathedrâ?" asked the Gallicans. "By this obvious sign," answered their opponents, "that whenever he is condemning a heresy ex cathedrâ, he expresses or implies an anathema on its wilful upholders." This phrase is in use to this day among Ultramontane controversialists, in the very same sense in which it was originally employed. When they say that the Pope is not speaking ex cathedrâ, unless he expresses or implies

* We may cite, as one proof out of many, a letter cited by Antoine (de Fide, c. 3, a. 5, s. 9), written to the Pope by the well-known Cardinal de Noailles, Archbishop of Paris, and subscribed by most (pluribus) of the French archbishops and bishops. "It was certain," says this letter, "to it [the French clerical body] that nothing is wanting to the Pontifical decrees against Jansenius, in order that they may *oblige the whole Church*. . . . I consider that the clergy would have made *the same profession* also concerning *the Apostolic definitions against Baius, Molinos, and the 'Maximes des Saints,'* had these been in question."—Now the condemnations of both Baius and Molinos contain many censures below that of heresy; while that of Fénélon's "Maximes des Saints" does not speak of heresy at all.

Fénélon, on the contrary, as being an Ultramontane, held as a matter of course, that the Pope's condemnation of his book was infallible, independently of any other Episcopal judgment; and this, be it again observed, on a matter where there was no question of *heresy* whatever, but only of minor error. See his words quoted by de Maistre ("du Pape," book i., c. 16) in a note.

an anathema,—nothing is further from their mind than what the objector supposes; viz., that he is not infallible in pronouncing censures lower than that of heretical: the question is not in their thoughts at all. What they mean is simply this: that the Pope is not *infallible* in denouncing some tenet as heretical, unless he so denounces it *ex cathedrâ;* and that such denunciation is not *ex cathedrâ*, unless an *anathema* be expressed or implied.

Such evidently is an *intelligible* account of the matter; and we are next to show that it is the true account. From the multitude of proofs which throng on our mind, we will select a very few.

1. We believe that, in every single instance, a careful study of the writer's general argument will show clearly the soundness of our interpretation. We have taken Perrone as our specimen: let us exhibit the proof therefore in his case. He at once appends this note to the passage which we quoted above:—

"Wherefore neither do personal facts, nor precepts, nor rescripts, nor opinions which the Roman Pontiffs from time to time express, nor disciplinary decrees, nor omissions of a definition, nor other very many things of the same kind, come under the head of these decrees concerning which we speak. For though all these things—considering the supreme authority from which they issue—should always be held in high estimation, and should be received with humble submission (*obsequio*) of mind and reverence, nevertheless they do not constitute that definition ex cathedrâ, of which we are speaking, and in which alone we maintain Pontifical infallibility. Compare the remarks, not less apt than prudent, made on this matter (after Canus and Bellarmine) by Pietro Ballerini, 'de vi ac ratione primatûs' (c. 15, s. 10)."

Of course, if Perrone had meant, as the objector supposes, to contrast the censure of tenets as *heretical*, with the censure of them merely as *unsound*,—if he had intended to say that the Pope is infallible in the former but not in the latter office,—such a circumstance must have occupied a prominent place in the above note; for certainly the Pope's fallibility in minor censures would be an immeasurably more important qualification, than his fallibility in precepts, and rescripts, and personal facts or opinions. Then, again, Perrone quotes a particular section of Ballerini, as expressing his own doctrine; but if you refer to that section, you will find that Ballerini therein distinctly implies the Pope's *in*fallibility in minor censures. (See n. 32 of the section.)

2. If the objector's interpretation were correct—if the question turned at all on the "object," and not merely on the "subject" of infallibility—the theologians on whom he rests would of course be equally anxious to add the same qualification, when they are speaking, not of the Pope's, but of the Church's infallibility. But, on the contrary, not one of them gives the slightest hint, that the Church's infallibility is limited to her condemnation of heresy. Or, rather, they expressly teach the contrary; as, *e. g.*, Perrone in the passage which we have quoted in p. 81.

3. It frequently happens that the Holy Father, in one and the same pronouncement, condemns a variety of propositions,—some as heretical, and others as unsound in a lesser degree. Nay, he does so more commonly, without even specifying which censure belongs to which proposition. According to the objector's interpretation of those theologians whom he cites, they teach that such a pronouncement is ex cathedrâ, so far as it condemns *heretical* proposi-

tions; but that the very same pronouncement is not ex cathedrâ, so far as it condemns propositions *unsound in a lesser degree.* Moreover, where the Pope does not particularly state which propositions are or are not heretical—as, *e.g.*, in the condemnation of Baius, of Molinos, and of Quesnel—they must further teach that the faithful have no means whatever of knowing, which part of the pronouncement is ex cathedrâ and which is otherwise. It is plainly impossible, that eminent and approved theologians can have taken up a position so obviously self-contradictory.

We might indefinitely prolong our reply, but have surely said enough. As to the positive ground for that thesis which we have maintained, we have adduced in previous numbers a sufficient array of reasons. Dr. Murray, in his treatise, has added very many more; and there is a large additional number in reserve, if wanted. Our present object has not been to add any positive argument, but to remove one particular objection.*

The case of Galileo has been again and again alleged, as by far the strongest and most irrefragable disproof of our thesis; and we entered on it, therefore, at considerable length. Principally we urged, that there is no pretence whatever for saying that the Pope condemned Copernicanism ex cathedrâ; or that even those most opposed to that theory, claimed the congregational decree as infallibly condemning it. To this, the one essential part of our argument, we have as yet heard no objection.

---

* This objection will be found more fully answered in the Preface.

But the further question, of doctrinal decrees issued by a Pontifical Congregation, is closely connected with the thesis which we had been treating; and it is one of much importance at the present time: for which reasons we thought it more satisfactory to discuss that question at length. We do not here speak of those doctrinal decrees, which issue indeed from the Congregations, but which are promulgated by the Pope's special command; because we are disposed to hold, with Zaccaria, that these pronouncements are ex cathedrâ (p. 130): and Pius IX.'s words (ibid.) seem strongly to support that proposition. Here, then, we are speaking of those doctrinal decrees, which may have received indeed his sanction, but which are not promulgated by his special command; and of which, therefore, no one has ever alleged that he issues them as Universal Teacher.

Now, of these, no less than of the others, Pius IX. has infallibly decreed (p. 120), that a Catholic man of science is bound to yield them his interior assent. The first question, then, concerns the *nature* of that assent; which differs in kind, as it is axiomatically evident, from that due to an infallible decision. We may thus illustrate its character: A youth of fourteen years old is being instructed by his father, to whom he has every reason for looking up, in the facts and principles of history. He accepts the whole instruction with unqualified assent; nor does the very thought of its being erroneous in any particular so much as enter his mind. Yet, if you pressed him with the question, he must reply that his father is not infallible, and that part of the paternal instruction may possibly be mistaken. The assent due from every

Catholic to the doctrinal decrees of a Pontifical Congregation is (we maintain) the same in kind, but very far firmer in degree—very far firmer in degree, for the various reasons assigned in pp. 134-137.

It is now admitted on all hands, that the condemnation of Copernicanism was (as one may say) objectively incorrect; that the theory, then declared contrary to the Scriptures, is not really contrary to them. Of this undoubted fact, two explanations are possible. The first is, that Paul V. and his advisers simply made a mistake; nor is there any insurmountable difficulty in such a supposition. The youthful son gains immeasurably more of real knowledge by accepting without hesitation the whole of his father's instruction, than he could possibly gain by questioning and sifting it, and believing nothing on his father's authority. In like manner, a Catholic would gain far more spiritual knowledge by interiorly accepting all these decrees, than by declining such acceptance; even though it might happen, on certain very rare occasions, that they led him into error.

But, for ourselves, we are most unwilling to admit that any doctrinal guidance is mistaken, which the Pope has put forth as Head of the Church; even though he has not given it in his capacity of Universal Teacher (see pp. 185-7). True, there is no *promise* of such inerrancy; and whenever a clear case of mistake is conclusively established, we will, of course, change our mind. But, at all events, for more than one reason, we thought it very important to point out what we consider unquestionable; viz., that Galileo's condemnation was no mistake at all, in any proper sense of that word.

If a decree is put forth claiming infallibility, it purports to have God's unfailing guarantee of its truth. But it is most certain that Galileo's condemnation was *not* put forth with any claim to infallibility; and we ask, therefore, what such a decree *does* purport to be. No answer but one can possibly be given, as a moment's consideration will evince. It purports to instruct Catholics in that conclusion, which legitimately follows from existing data. Now, we argued at much length, that the contrariety of Copernicanism to Scripture *was* the consequence legitimately resulting from the data of 1616. (See pp. 140-152; 160; 182.) The reason why Copernicanism is now justly held to be consistent with Scripture, is its having been scientifically established (p. 142-3); but, so far was this from having been the case in Galileo's time, that, on the contrary, as a matter of mere science, its falsehood was more probable than its truth (pp. 146-152). Nor was Galileo's confidence in the scientific strength of his theory any presumption of its real strength; because the one main argument on which he laid his stress, is now admitted by every one to have been absolutely worthless (p. 400). By accident he was right; but, "formally," even as a man of science, he was wrong.

The decree purported to be—not infallibly guaranteed by God, but—the true conclusion from existing data. Well, it *was* the true conclusion from existing data: how, therefore, in any true sense, can it be called mistaken? On the contrary, it afforded "true doctrinal guidance to contemporary Catholics" (p. 186). For (1) it inculcated on them that doctrinal lesson, which legitimately resulted from existing data;

and (2) it warned them against "a most false, proud, irreverent, and dangerous principle of Scriptural interpretation." What is that principle? "The contradicting the obvious and traditional sense of Scripture, on the strength of a theory scientifically unlikely." And this is a principle as anti-Catholic now as it was then.

This then is the point which we wished to make clear. Before we were aware of any adverse criticism on our article, we felt that we had not sufficiently explained our meaning, where we had spoken of "true doctrinal guidance being afforded to contemporary Catholics." Of this, however, we hope we have now given a sufficient elucidation.

We may conclude by mentioning, that those astronomers who advocated the Copernican *hypothesis*, as the one most serviceable for advancing their science, not only were never discouraged in Rome, but were more favoured there than their opponents. Our authority for this statement is a very interesting letter addressed, three or four years ago, to the *Tablet* by Professor Robertson.

THE END.

COX AND WYMAN, PRINTERS, GREAT QUEEN STREET, LINCOLN'S-INN-FIELDS.

www.ingramcontent.com/pod-product-compliance
Lightning Source LLC
Chambersburg PA
CBHW030312270326
41926CB00010B/1335
* 9 7 8 3 7 4 1 1 7 6 0 8 1 *